The first book in the series
written by Nicole Beecher

How To Get Th
Beauty The

Book One:

Recruitment essentials for all Beauty Students and Beauty Therapists

Book Two:
Advanced Considerations: Recruitment Secrets for
Experienced Beauty Therapists

Published by Beauty Recruitment Publishing

Beauty Recruitment Publishing.
P/O Box 541, Guildford, GU3 3XS

Please Read

The author has done her best to present accurate and up-to-date
information in this book, but she cannot guarantee that the
information is correct or will suit your particular situation. This
book is sold with the understanding that the publisher and the
author are not engaged in rendering legal, accounting or any other
professional services. If expert assistance is required, the services of
a competent professional should be sought.

How To Get The Best Beauty Therapy Jobs

Recruitment secrets for Beauty Therapists

Book One

Recruitment essentials for all Beauty Students and Beauty Therapists

Written By

Nicole Beecher

Published By

Beauty Recruitment Publishing

Contents

The Essential Guide to Getting the Best Beauty Therapy Jobs

Introduction

For all Beauty Therapists, Beauty Students and Newly Qualified Therapists.

This series of books is different from any other beauty career series; it covers dilemmas and situations that happen. Whether you use job boards or agencies or go it alone in your search, this is information that you need to support you.

Written from the view point of what really works and does not work in securing the best job possible in the beauty industry, this book is about getting the best positions, the most money, and the best career prospects to fit your life style. It is not designed to be politically correct. It is written from the experience of knowing what companies want, who they take on and why. It is about making the most of your unique situation. It is written with your long-term "future proofing" prospects in mind; because some of your careers will span many changes in your life time, and those changes need to be taken into account when giving advice. It is written knowing that most of you will want different things at different times of your life and that you are individuals.

This Essential Guide to your career in the Beauty Industry is aimed at covering your journey throughout your career. It serves as a step-by-step guide once you have made a decision to get a new job, and also a reference book that you dip into for particular guidance during your career. You can refer back to this book long after you have finished college, are changing jobs, or moving up in your career ladder.

This book covers all of the questions, issues and decisions you have to make when embarking on a new job, explanations on the different job search methods you can apply, the positive and negative aspects of each method. There is advice on how to make the most out of Agencies, Job Boards, Direct Applications. Plus a tried and tested formula for writing your CV to achieve the most effective responses. Find out how to explain difficult episodes in your career, how to decide in which direction to move your career; how to avoid making mistakes; plus many, many, more tips, advice and amusing real-life examples that Therapists and Salons have experienced.

All of the names have been changed and the new names picked purely for rhyming reasons!

The second and advanced book in the "How To Get The Best Beauty Therapy Jobs" series continues the frank advice and guidance as you make the journey through your career and is suitable for experienced and senior therapists.

1

A Salon's Worst Nightmare

Job-Hopping Jane

This is the story of Jane

Jane is ambitious, that's true, and loyal, if only she could find the right salon to be loyal to. She is experienced, in a multiple, short-burst kind of way, and it is true she does have a considerable work history spanning more than 101 salons, no kidding! She is the Serial Therapist. Yes, she does have knowledge of a wide range of products that she has used – but never actually had formal training in any of the product houses in fifteen years of working as a Beauty Therapist.

Jane's CV begins:–
"Jane, an ambitious and very confident Senior Beauty Therapist, with fifteen years' experience in the industry, and a wide variety of product experience. A loyal reliable therapist, a good team member, able to work alone, looking for a professional salon where she can have a career path to management".

Unaccountably, according to Jane, she has had a run of bad luck with her jobs. It is not her fault, it is a complete mystery. The reasons vary and none of the salons has fulfilled the promises made at interview; in one case, the hours were not what she had been told; in another, the salon was not professional enough; in another; the owner was rude, and in another, the pay was not enough. Expanding on the rude salon-owner Jane wails, "it is just not right to speak to someone in that way, is it?" She doesn't wait for a response and continues "Who do they think they are, I have far more experience than they ever had". Jane continues "It's not my fault I was sick that day and then late the next and the train broke down the third day, admittedly, that was a bit of bad luck, but it wasn't my fault."

Then Jane decides to become a Beauty Therapist "Temp" working for various Temp Agencies. After all, with all of her experience she considers she will be able to earn a fortune, choose the hours she works and be her own boss. Perfect!

The Agencies are delighted with such an experienced Temp coming on to their books. Her CV has been written in such away that her unfortunate experiences are not revealed; if they had, there would not be a CV long enough to cover her entire career to date.

However, her sad tale of woes continues into her new career as a Temp.

Jane complains to her friend; "The journey was just too far, what was the Temp Agency thinking of, sending me there", so she didn't go back on Saturday, "Well, would you?", she said. Yes she admits, it was their busiest day but she didn't feel bad because they were horrible to her… and, so on.

If only she could find the right salon to be loyal to, but none of the salons is professional enough for her. It takes a while for Jane to work her way through all of the Temp Agencies before they have all experienced the fallout from her trail of unhappy customers. Jane knows everything there is to know about any beauty salon you care to pick in London. If she hasn't worked there, then she has probably had an interview there, and she probably turned the job down.

Jane has a personal and in-depth knowledge of every Beauty Job Agency, and knows most of the salons on their books anyway. Sadly, she has run out of places to work. But it's okay! Jane is nothing if not resourceful and she has a great new idea! She changes her CV, mainly out of necessity and to save some trees (due to the number of pages it needed to fit all of her jobs in) and she proudly announces "I have made a 'generic' CV", which, it has to be said, was a masterpiece in hiding the truth, and managing to convey fifteen years of experience without mentioning one single job in two pages.

Armed with her new CV, Jane can now apply via the Job Boards for unsuspecting salons to receive her CV, because she wasn't having much success with the agencies who all, miraculously, seem to be very quiet on the jobs front, much to her surprise.

Fortunately Jane is an extreme example, but an absolutely genuine one. She has never managed to hold down a steady job for more than a couple of months. She has been a temp on and off for many years and because she has never been in any location for very long she has not received any product training.

Yet she is a strong character and very challenging in her approach to salon owners.

Jane has a fantastic ability to get herself interviews. She is funny, warm, friendly, independent, great on the telephone and face-to-face meetings, and can win over people easily. She is an okay therapist but not a natural and not into the advanced treatments. Really she missed her vocation in life, she would have been great at selling and could have used her beauty qualifications to sell in the beauty industry. Never one to give up, Jane's sense of ambition and her sense of humour remain intact to this day, her aspirations continue albeit in a different direction . . . she wants to become a beauty teacher, for the time being anyway!

Why is Jane at the start of this book? Jane made so many mistakes in her career and you can avoid every one of them by using this book to guide you throughout your career as a therapist. Use it to check how to deal with job situations, when you are going for an interview, when you want to search for a new job, when you want to write your CV, or if you just want to check your own thinking about a situation.

If you are an experienced therapist then your requirements from this book will be different to those of the College leaver and your interview may have a different approach. Accordingly some of the advice is marked as being particularly for experienced or newly qualified therapists.

Both experienced Therapists and College leavers will benefit from some of the chapters on presentation, salon expectations, CVs and methods of searching for a job, as well as the examples of mistakes made by therapists during interviews.

This book will take you from College days through to your first job and it will be useful to refer back to throughout your career. Further on in your career, when more advanced negotiating skills, are required the second book in this series will take you through the next steps.

2

Getting Started on Your Job Search from your armchair

The First and a Vital Stage of your Search

Read this paragraph if you are already employed or already experienced and looking to move jobs

First of all, list your priorities. Consider the following questions:

What it is you want to get out of your new job that you are not getting in your current job?

This is really important to those of you in this category, because there is no point in moving for the sake of moving. If you are unhappy, ask yourself why are you unhappy. Is it money, location, not enough variety of treatments, are you stagnant in your job? Do you want a bigger or smaller environment? Perhaps you don't like your boss or colleagues or perhaps you want to move your career into a different direction? Or maybe you are being forced to move jobs for reasons out of your control? Maybe it's the hours or maybe your personal circumstances have changed and it's not fitting in? It is okay to have more than one priority.

Write your reasons down. Be honest. If it's because you want to live near your boyfriend then write it down on the list. Nobody else needs to see this list. You will refer to it later so keep it handy, and add to it as and when you think of things that are important to you. Sometimes these thoughts do not come to mind on demand.

Read this paragraph if you are a College Leaver: First job:

You need to consider to where you would like your career path to take you.

Before you decide, your first task is to read the chapters in this book on the different types of career paths within the beauty industry. You may find that this will also help you if you are in the lucky position of having to decide which job to take for your first one. If you have several job offers, and you are set on a career path to take you to Spa Management, on that basis you may decide to head straight to a spa for your first job.

To College Leavers in particular, it is a good idea to "future proof" your career and this means not limiting your options for the long term. At some stage you could decide that you want to change to a salon environment, or you may decide you want to have your own business, or move to more clinical or medical areas. The economic market could change in a way that means you have to be more open and willing to work on other jobs rather than specialise in order to get work. By giving yourself a strong foundation, you will be able to choose and move at any time in your career to other sectors rather than leaving college and immediately restricting yourself for the future by leaving behind some of your skills.

It is better to get a position, if you can at this stage in your career, that uses as many, if not all, of your skills learnt at college, where you will really become proficient at your treatments, learn new salon techniques, build up your speed, become experienced at client liaison and care. This first job is often considered a kind of finishing school. If you can find one, it is better to join a salon or spa that can support and help you as you find your confidence in the salon environment and which has the infrastructure to offer guidance on how to deal with situations and problems that may occur as you are finding your feet. If you are lucky enough to find such a salon, then you will find this first year or two will be a good foundation for the rest of your career and contribute to an excellent CV.

This paragraph is for both College Leavers and Experienced Therapists

Now you should start thinking about what you can bring to the table. If you are experienced you can look back over the jobs that you have had, and think about the parts of the job you excelled at, the bits you liked and the bits that were a challenge! What, if any, of those experiences would you like to utilise in your new job? What can you offer to your potential new company? This is going to help when you focus on your CV. Make notes and keep them ready for when you put your CV together. (You have already started your preparation for your CV by making these notes and thinking about what you want; you are not wasting time.)

Once you have decided on your priorities then you can focus your approach to your job search according to the job sector you are heading towards. You will have some preparation to do before you apply for the jobs, and you should spend some time on this before you start applying.

You will need to prepare your CV and be ready for Interviews and Trade Tests. This next section will focus on the preparation. There is a tried-and-tested chapter on the best CV layout for you to copy and use, and tips to get the best out of yourself; it is not easy to write about oneself, this formula is the most effective layout used to get a job in the beauty industry. Do your CV well now and you will never have to do it again, apart from updating as you move through your career. So if you put the effort in now, you can consider the time-consuming part of the CV a job done for ever more! It should be pointed out at this stage that you must still re-read your CV each time you update it, This may seem obvious but a huge number of CVs that are put forward for jobs have just had the last position added. Clearly without the candidate reading it. The problem occurs when you are changing direction slightly, which could happen several times during your career and this can diminish the impact of your CV, confusing the person reading it as to what your objective is.

Confusing Karen

Karen sent in her CV to a company in response to an advertisement for a Sales role. Within her CV it mentioned that on a previous job she wanted to move out of Sales and go into Training; as she did not feel Sales was for her. On her application form it said that currently she is a Teacher.

When interviewing her, the company opened up the interview by asking why she was applying for a sales role when she had clearly stated that she did not enjoy sales on her CV. This meant that Karen started the interview on a negative note; and it got worse as she hastened to improvise in an attempt to show it was not all sales that she disliked, and she explained that it was that particular job rather than sales in general. Which then unfortunately took her down a route of sounding negative about a previous employer, which was mistake number three.

The point of this example is not only the resulting negative interview; it is to explain the butterfly effect of not checking your CV when updating.

Of course another possible consequence of not checking your CV is that you don't get invited for an interview at all!

3

Continuing Easy Preparation for your Ultimate CV

You have started the preparation and are already well on the way.

Many people find it difficult to make their own CV. Most people hate writing about themselves and find it difficult to be objective. Very often they get other people to write it for them and often that person, whilst helping them, may come from a different industry and will not understand the right tone for the beauty industry nor what is important, or the appropriate terminology.

Some people do not give the time and attention to their CV and in their hurry to apply for a job, rattle off any old thing or, just as bad, copy an example from another industry and cut and paste it into an email. Included in this chapter are the reasons why you should approach a CV in a certain way and what things should be avoided.

When you understand the impact and effect of these things you will have the information for life. This will make it easier for future CVS because all of a sudden it seems obvious. The Ultimate CV is the very best and simplest form of CV for your job as a Beauty Therapist. You will find in this chapter every aspect of writing the CV and examples of possible stumbling blocks you may come across whilst writing it.

One such stumbling block; so often, when writing a CV, it is the smallest thing that manages to stop us from finishing it, which then stops us from applying for that great job. Which then might leave us feeling disappointed with ourselves and that makes us go and buy that extra bar of chocolate; go shopping because we need a treat; oh no! now we've put on weight, are getting into debt and declaring ourselves fed up and depressed!

All this because we got stuck on whether to own up on our CV to that 'one-week placement' that went wrong; and all that unnecessary worry that put us in a negative mood and worse, because forever more we deem ourselves as having something supposedly shameful to hide in our CV.

The advice here is that whatever that shameful thing, it will be far worse in your mind than it actually is. The old adage that "the fear is greater than the reality" is true. Plus we are all very self-critical and your little mistake or, as I prefer to say, "lesson in experience" is just a little blip in your life. Rest assured the person reading your CV or interviewing you will have made their own blips in their careers. If they hadn't then we would all be perfect robots, and there wouldn't be any clients because they would all be perfect as well, so then there wouldn't be a job and a boss to interview you!

This CV is written with experience of what works and doesn't work in the presentation of a CV to an employer in the Beauty Industry. Of course you can always cherry-pick parts of The Ultimate CV formula and adapt them to your own ideas, and you will be able to refer to this section as some parts become more relevant as you move through your career.

There is a check list at the end of this chapter to assist you in remember the points when making your CV.

4

The Ingredients, Recipe and Method for the Ultimate CV

A step-by-step guide to putting your CV together, proven method, no guessing. References; who, why, where, so what? and a true-life example of why a reference changed the life of one Therapist.

Moving on to the next stage in your preparation for your CV.

Don't do it in a hurry.

If you are an Experienced Beauty Therapist, plan for it to take you at least three days to make your CV, particularly if you have had several jobs or careers. Don't panic, they don't have to be consecutive days but if you allow for it to take time you won't get so stressed or make mistakes and you only have to add to it in the future, so do it well and it's *predominantly* a job done for life!

If you are a College Leaver on your first job from college you will not need to allow quite so long.

Why are mistakes on a CV even more of a problem than before?

Mistakes on CVs are more of a problem now than ever before because people store your CVs on computers, particularly when you apply on line, and they will often keep all the different versions you send.

It is also more of a problem because the ease with which we can send our CVs by email means that an evening of 'CV sending', with a glass of wine at hand, can mean 1000s of people reading your CV the following morning. If you are applying on several Job Boards, those people may have your CV emailed to them many times over. So what appeared a good idea; "hic!" at the time may not seem so funny in the morning when you spot that glaring error in the spelling of Curriculum Vitae (yes it happens a lot), or your current boss notices your details on the web. Though one could argue that's not a bad thing if you want to leave anyway! However, you might have preferred to have chosen your exit timing and you might not have chosen those words if you had known that (a) your boss was going to read it, and (b) you were under the influence of wine-induced boldness and (c) you want a reference.

As you work through the process there is an explanation as to why each section is important, why you have to make such an effort to find all the information you require. If you're wondering and feeling that is it worth the effort, you can't be bothered, or its too much trouble and boring, this may help you to understand and help you to focus on the end result whilst you are going through old drawers for bits of paper, contemplating going in the loft, garage or wardrobe or maybe just needing a little extra courage or tenacity to make phone calls to old past companies or colleges for the information.

Day One

Find your College Certificates and photocopy several copies of each one. If you don't have a copier at home or access to one through family or friends then you can normally find one at libraries, print shops or similar. This can be expensive as you will be charged per copy but it is worth the cost ten times over throughout your career.

If you have any Product Training Certificates do the same with those.

Three very good reasons for taking copies of both:

❶ You will find that it is useful to always have copies available in case you suddenly see the most fantastic job advertised and need to apply in a hurry.

❷ Keep your original certificates safe and never ever give them to a salon to hang on their wall. You can give the salon one of your photo copies if they want them.

There are so many examples of Therapists who hand over their "Original" Certificates to their new boss to put on the wall. Then they have a problem when they want to get a new job, want to show their certificates and can't ask their boss for them without giving the game away. Worse, if you were given the sack and were marched out of the salon for some dreadful unimaginable deed, you might not remember in the heat of the moment to ask for your Certificates. Then you would have to go back red-faced and get them, if they still had them!

❸ It is not unheard of for colleges to close and so you cannot rely on getting copies at a later date.

Make a list of any product training you have received, including the dates. There is a very useful section at the back of this book for keeping records of dates and names of courses.

Two very good reasons for this:

❶ This will then be ready for when you build your CV and it is also useful to keep to hand for when you are speaking to agencies or companies because you will be able to rattle off your training without forgetting any details. Add to the list as you receive further product training throughout your career.

❷ Having the dates of courses on your CV is a nice touch; it certainly makes an impression when they are there. It tells the salon if they will need to update you on a particular product course and it tells them something about you, that you have attention to detail, and are organised and efficient. More than that, it tells them you have an appreciation of the courses you have been given by a previous employer.

This last point is important because it indicates to the salon owner that you will care about her/his costs and overheads and appreciate it when he/she invests in you. It shows that you put a value to the time and effort and money invested in that course. The extension to this is that because you appreciate the product training you have received you therefore don't just "expect it as your right".... therefore the salon owner can see that you are not only a much nicer and considerate person to have working for them, and less of a challenge, but also someone who has an understanding of cost implications in a business and hopefully your CV might be put in the "to consider" pile.

Keeping a Record of Training Costs

It is also a good idea to keep a record of the cost of courses, travel, and accommodation in the section at the back of this book so that you can easily refer back to costs at any time. This can be useful for several situations. If a company is paying for the course and you need to claim the cost back, if you are self-employed and need to claim against your tax, or if you have a "tie in" clause with a salon in your contract of employment and you have to pay back the cost of a course or a percentage of any training costs, should you leave within a certain period of time. Normally a year but can be longer or shorter. Not all salons have this clause and some will only apply it at their discretion.

Get a hard backed File or plastic report file with compartments and put your copies of certificates into it so that you have a very nice show case to take with you to interviews (as well as an excellent way of keeping your copies safe). You can add to this throughout your career. It is also a good idea to keep in it for your own peace of mind a copy of your CV on paper, memory stick or CD or similar, and your list of product training with dates. So if you move house, country, job, or have an unexpected interview, you have it all there.

So many people make the excuse that they have just moved house and their computer is not working yet so they don't have a copy of their CV and have lost their certificates, causing missed opportunities and frustration. This also says to the person wanting your CV that you are not really serious about your job search.

If you make your file and treat it as you would your passport, a vital document that you need to keep safe and whose location is never a mystery, you will always be prepared.

Get a good photograph taken

This is a contentious subject and you don't have to do it, but for the Ultimate CV it should be included. It is apparently not politically correct and some people take offence when asked for it. In fact, at the time of writing this book, in some situations it may even be unlawful for a potential employer to ask for a photograph on application, and so nowadays not everyone will ask.

This is the beauty industry however, and it is about image, looks, feeling good, health etc. It does not matter if you are 18 or 80, the employer wants to see that you are presentable and will represent their company in what ever capacity you are applying for.

More importantly there will always be people that will put their photo on the CV and if an employer has two CVs, one with a photo and one without, which one is going to be more memorable? Why not give yourself an advantage. If someone can see your picture it is true that they immediately make a few assumptions about you and so there is one very important point to remember if you go down the photograph route. Have it taken in uniform or very smart business clothes, depending on the job you are applying for, and if possible avoid the latest trend to take your own photograph with your computer, web cam or mobile phone camera. It just results in that slightly sideways and strangely staring eyes look. That is not a positive dynamic image.

It is astonishing that so many people have a photograph taken in their night clubbing gear or worse, they have been to one of these image studios that do a fantastic make over and present them with a photograph that comes out with a semi-porn mouth pout and which is completely different to their normal daily look.

Apart from not giving the right image if you do get an interview they want to recognise the person walking through the door. A photograph in a pristine uniform or a smart suit, with your hair tidy and just the right amount of make up, looking professional and confident will go a long way to getting you that job.

The other mistake people make is sending in a holiday snap of them on a balcony in some exotic location with a lovely pink flower in their hair, holding a glass of something bubbly, looking lovely, tanned, happy. No doubt in their mind a very good picture which they imagine makes them look well-travelled, sophisticated and beautiful.

Unfortunately it is sending out the wrong message. You want that top job, you want them to know you are a professional and health-conscious adviser, a guru of the beauty industry who is respected by her peers and offers a top-notch service. The very image of pureness with a self-controlled healthy lifestyle. Someone who your clients would like to aspire to!

Okay so this may be stretching the realms of reality, but that holiday picture is saying "this is Sally who goes to Spain and enjoys a glass wine, sunbathes and parties and looks like a nice person, just like one of my friends really, and is happy for everyone to know about her personal life." What you want it to say is, "here is a professional person who I would be happy to have a treatment with and to ask her advice. This person has worked hard for her qualifications and is a credit to her profession."

If you are going for a sales job you should have the picture taken in a suit and for Senior Sales and Product House Management jobs, it is worth considering hiring a professional photographer.

Gathering: Day Two

A small paragraph to those of you on your first job

This section on CVs is not so hard for you. At this stage in your career, you don't have to put nearly as much effort into the "gathering of information" as you will later on in life. Therefore you can put even more effort into the presentation. So why doesn't this happen? I have seen thousands of CVs from students and college leavers that are not good, and could do better!

The only answer I can come up with is that it is one of those strange things about life that it is only when you are older that you will realise that doing your

CV now is the easiest it will ever be, and of course, they haven't read my book!

Back to gathering:

Gather together all of your information. This is often not easy to find and inevitably what happens is that by the time you have managed to find all the information, you have then run out of energy, oomph, creative flow, or just time in order to make the CV and you end up not taking such care over the finished article, a large glass of wine is beckoning and all sorts of funny things get put down, particularly when it gets to the "hobbies and interests" bit.

The information you require is: **Dates and Names.**

Start and finish date of your Beauty College and the Name of the College.

The start and finish date of education if applicable and the Name of the School.

The start and finish date of each job if applicable and the Name of the Company.

It is vital that you include the months as well as the year. It is not acceptable to put just the year and, worse than that, it makes people think you are hiding something.

I have had many CVs presented to me with just a year put against a job and I have come to the conclusion that this is normally because the person concerned just could not be bothered and did not realise the consequences of their lack of attention to detail.

This is how it will look to the person reading the CV, one or possibly all of the following:

- ❂ You can't be bothered.
- ❂ You are disorganised.
- ❂ You do not make an effort.
- ❂ You do not have attention to detail.
- ❂ You must be hiding something and are being evasive.

PHEW!

Did you realise that that little slip sent so many thought patterns through the mind of the person reading your CV?

And I haven't even finished on dates yet! The Beauty College date is probably one of the most important dates on the CV in reality and it is often missed out. You must have the Start date and the Finish date; Month and Year of your college.

The person reading your CV will first look to see when you qualified, where you qualified and what your qualifications are. They will not want to hunt for it, or to work it out by process of elimination. If they have to do that they are already finding you awkward or complicated or someone who doesn't want to make it clear when they qualified. Worse, they may think that again you are hiding something and you did not finish the course. Here are some of the thoughts that may cross that person's mind.

You are too casual about your CV, what does that say about you? Or maybe you are just disorganized, but that's not good either. Maybe you are being deliberately evasive? Perhaps you dropped out of college early or didn't pass your exams?

They may have several CVs to read and immediately they will have a negative feeling towards yours as they will have to work out the date or ask you. The point is, why should they and why would they? They are busy people with lots of other great CVs from Beauty Therapists that have taken care to present exactly the information that the person needs in order to decide who to short list for interview. You may actually be a better Beauty Therapist, more suitable, a nicer person even, but you have missed that opportunity to prove it.

Jobs – Remember at this stage that you are just making a list not the final CV, so write down all the jobs and dates

If you are Newly Qualified, it is good to put in any work experience you have had at college and any Saturday or Holiday jobs you have achieved at school or college.

For the person with a career history, list your jobs, all of them, even ones that you may not include in the final CV.

List just the company name and location. You don't need the full address, just the Town or City.

List your job titles against the applicable jobs and the dates you started and left.

Jot down against each job on a bit of paper why you left. Write it as it is, just a couple of lines, this is for your eyes only at this stage and so it is just a memory jogger.

References – Get together referees' names

If you are newly qualified and on your first job with no holiday work then it can be a good idea to put down a professional person in your life such as a teacher or long-standing senior family friend.

If you are experienced then you can put down ideally one or two previous employers and I think it is always useful to also have a senior family friend or acquaintance or professional person as a personal reference, not just someone you have worked for.

I say this because of a most remarkable experience I had once with a candidate who applied to me to work abroad. Until this point I will admit I had not put too much store on personal references and this close encounter with disaster changed my view completely, on behalf of a therapist and a client who nearly missed employing an excellent employee.

This Therapist had an impressive CV, her interview confirmed she was a very professional person; we were very impressed with her and above all liked her very much. Her trade test had been tailored specifically for the salon concerned and she came out as 100% capable and in short a great therapist, totally suited to working abroad, steady and straight forward.

Everything had been agreed in principle for her to join the company abroad and references and certificates had been submitted to apply for her Visa. There was a delay on the Criminal Report Check that she had been asked to obtain from the police for the Visa; this was typically taking anything up to about two months at the time. In this case it was taking longer and was delaying her starting her new job.

Out of the blue came a phone call from the prospective employer abroad saying they would not be employing her after all. They said that they had followed up on the references and had decided not to make an offer as they felt she was of bad character.

Alarm bells were ringing, something did not feel right about this and the Agent rang back the salon owner and asked them to expand on their reasons for rejection. (After some cajoling and it was only because of a long-standing relationship between our two companies that they agreed to discuss it.)

It would appear that the salon had received a call from a gentleman who had made them promise that they would not tell the therapist about his call. The Salon had no idea how he knew about the job as they had only dealt with the candidate and her Agent.

This man advised the Salon not to employ this candidate, warning them that she had lied about her health, had financial issues and had "fixed" her medical certificate, implying that she was not only unhealthy, would take a lot of time off sick, but could not be trusted and was hiding financial problems, that were of a dubious nature. Plus her references were all made up and had been written by her.

Her Agents had such a strong feeling about this that they decided to risk the relationship with their client and just said "Rubbish". They did not believe it at all. The Salon, having dealt with the Agent for many years, had respect for their judgement was willing to be proved wrong.

The Agent and the Salon agreed that by revealing the name of this person making the claims to the Agent and not directly to the Therapist, the salon had not compromised its promise to the man to keep his phone call secret. The agent had no such agreement with the man; the Agent's responsibility was to their client, the Salon and their candidate, so they were within their rights to discuss it. The Agent did not have to adhere to this agreement; as they had not made the promise. It would have been unfair to turn her down for the job because of this.

After investigations it turned out that this mystery caller was someone who until that point was considered a family friend, and someone whom she had previously lived with and who had only the day before been at her family home with her family having a Sunday lunch and sharing the celebrations of her imminent job.

Apparently this man had been causing her a few problems and so she had not, until that family lunch, mentioned her job abroad. On that day she announced her plans in the belief that it was all going ahead.

She was unaware that he had already made that mischief-making call and unaware that he already knew about the job.

Later on, she was to find out that he had actually discovered her plans for the job abroad because the police report had inadvertently been posted to the house that she had previously shared with him. He had hidden the police report, which had caused the delay in her receiving it, read it and it had given him the information that she was going abroad. The seed was planted in his mind that he could use the delay of the report to add to the salon's growing concern that it had not arrived. By damaging her character, he would make them put the two together and feel that she was a bad investment.

There were two reference names on her CV; one a previous employer and one a personal senior family friend. There were two written references; one was a salon owner who was on maternity leave.

The salon abroad, in reaction to the mischief-maker's call, had phoned to verify the written references they had been given.

They had not had a reply as the name on one reference was a lady on maternity leave and the other person was away on holiday.

The personal reference was a friend of the family who had known her since she was a little girl, who was of some standing in the community.

The Agent traced the salon owner on maternity leave and explained the situation and she confirmed that everything that was in the original reference was correct and she then wrote a letter to the Agent with a very nice reference that very day and faxed it over to the salon abroad.

When the Agent phoned the gentleman who was the Personal Reference and asked him if he would be prepared to write a reference, he was already on the case; he had just been speaking with the company abroad, having taking immediate action on hearing what had happened.

He confirmed that the salon was confident in his personal reference and that whilst he was on the phone to them they had received the faxed copy of the other salon's reference.

This was a team effort; but had she not had such fantastic referees, including a personal referee and a great agency, she would never have known why she had been turned down and an injustice would have been done.

I have shortened this story in order to protect the names and because it is not necessary to go into all of the details of how we got to the bottom of this in order to make my point that not only can a personal reference be very useful but it is also worth thinking hard about the person you put down. Your best friend of the week from work may not remember you in five years' time and they may not be able to impress a potential employer if need be.

Another example of why you should think carefully about who your friends are.

A French company approached an Agency to find them a Sales Manager for a new operation they were opening in Central London. The agency found them three excellent candidates, one of whom they were particularly keen on and the French Head Office would have offered her the job without meeting, based on their agents confidence in her.

However, at the last minute it was discovered that one of the executives for the French company was visiting London that weekend and they decided it would be good if she could meet this candidate.

It turned out they had worked with each other before and the meeting went very well and was lots of fun. The candidate reported back to her Agent that the interview went very well, that the person interviewing her had been a previous associate that she got on well with, and who knew her excellent track record in sales. In fact they had laughed about the competition they would have in sales when working together again. She was confident she had the job.

She was turned down for the job; the report from the Head Office came back to the Agency that the person interviewing her had said she was not the right sort of person for their company, in very hushed tones, the implication being that she was the wrong calibre of person, too brash.

The person they took on was not nearly as experienced and whilst the agency chose not to pass on the reasons for the decline of the job, it was fairly clear that this was a personal issue of the interviewer rather than anything to do with the candidate.

The other point to consider when putting down names for references. If you put down a friend at work as your reference and not the salon owner or boss, it opens up the question "why?" and makes the person reading your CV think that you may have had a problem with the boss, or maybe you were asked to leave. So where possible put down your employer for the work reference.

Day Three

Putting it all together – Now for the good bit, you have your information, dates, job lists, references and certificates and are ready to go

You will need to put a statement about yourself; this **is the single most important paragraph you will write in your CV**. It is the eye-catcher and it is more often than not the paragraph that gets you the interview.

This is where you can overcome any other issues in your CV by making an impact statement that tells them about you, your personality, what you can bring to the table and what you are looking for.

It is the paragraph where you say what you want to achieve, and it is here that you need to be clear. In Chapter 2, I asked you to consider what you want out of your new job and to make a list. This is where you will refer to that list, with regard to what you want out of your new job and what particular skills and benefits you can bring to the table.

It is also here that some people make a mistake; they write what they think someone wants to hear, without the knowledge to back it up at interview. Or they turn up for the interview saying something completely different from that indicated on their supporting statement.

Written as an opening statement on a Therapists CV:–

"An experienced therapist with 5 years experience, ambitious and looking for a progressive company to move my career forwards. Looking for full-time work in the London area".

Sounds great, until she turned up for the interview and said she did not want to work on Saturdays and only wanted part-time, because she has private clients.

None of which is a problem in itself, it is just that she portrayed herself as a different person, and their expectations were raised, so they were confused when she spoke. This left them feeling negative towards her and disappointed.

If she had said in her opening statement what she wanted, they may still have interviewed her, because she had the right amount of experience for them and there is often more than one position available in a Salon. Often it is the personality that counts and so, for the right person, they might have been flexible on full time or part time. (This is one area where an agency can be helpful.)

How long should your CV be?

Keep your CV as concise as possible and preferably to a maximum of two pages. If you are newly qualified, don't do the reverse and try to fill up two pages with big letters and unnecessary information. It is not needed to plump it out; one page is fine if you have not had any jobs before.

Don't write out unnecessary explanations for the obvious and repeat them word for word, over and over again for each job role. It will look exactly as if you don't know what to say and think you just have to fill up space.

Also, there are some parts of Beauty Therapy that are expected and practically included in the title and so do not need an explanation. Then to repeat the same explanation is almost an insult to the reader and takes up too much room on your CV.

Is it useful to have jobs out of the industry on your CV?

Yes I believe it is, this is contrary I know to what most people would advise but there are occasions when perhaps you may be going for a Beauty Therapy position and have a background for example in Nursing, Secretarial or Reception or even selling Loo Rolls! There are many examples of jobs that could be useful and the person interviewing you might be sizing you up for future projects that they are not in a position to mention now. Your experience in other industries might show something about your personality that is of interest.

So you have to weigh it up when you are writing your CV according to the space you have and decide if there is anything that really must be included that is from your previous experience.

What design or layout should you choose?

There are some fantastic-looking CVs out there and some real works of art but the most effective is actually very simple to produce and with regards to the beauty industry this is a tried-and-tested formula that works.

Lay out your CV in the order of this Ten Point Plan

1. Put your Name at the top and Curriculum Vitae

2. Put a photograph alongsside personal details.

3. Then put in a text box containing a paragraph about yourself and perhaps including what position and type of company you are looking for, and some key aspects of your personality.

4. After your text box you could put in 4 or 5 bullet points containing your strengths.

5. Next put a section on your Beauty Training Qualifications, college and dates.

⑥ Next your product training.

⑦ Then put in your career history.

⑧ If you have any particular achievements either include them with the relevant job text or put them under their own heading before hobbies.

⑨ Then your hobbies and interests.

⑩ Followed by Reference details.

Type Face

The most important thing to remember is to use a type face that is easy to read. Clear, simple and professional looking fonts are essential for your CV.

For the Ultimate CV use the "Arial Font" size 10 or 12 depending on how much you have to fit on your CV.

Arial is the most effective type face for our "Ultimate CV". Diane Simpson, a well-known authority on hand writing and type faces for effective marketing, once advised me that Arial is the most attractive to the eye and more effective to the 25 to 50 age group of decision-makers and I have always followed this little gem of information. See www.dianesimpson.co.uk.

Design
✪ Make sure it looks at its best in Black and White.
✪ Avoid lots of colours and background patterns.

If this is to be emailed, lots of background will slow the opening of the email. It may look fantastic on your colour printer, but the chances are the person printing it will be printing in black and white and so it may lose its effectiveness if it has been designed with colour in mind.

✪ Some CVs are so fussy it takes a good few seconds to find the key information. You can lose the reader's interest in that time.

✪ Some people use faxes and while you may email your CV to someone, they may fax it to their partner, boss, client etc, which is another reason why it needs to look good in black and white.

Common mistakes made with type face on a CV

Using capitals all the way through the CV is bad form because:

✪ It is considered rude.

✪ It is hard to read.

✪ It takes up too much space.

✪ It will make you appear to have bad reading and writing skills.

✪ It does not draw attention to the important aspects of your CV.

✪ The receiver of your CV is very likely not to read it.

✪ Ornate text or italics are harder to read and best avoided.

Emails

Again, avoid capitals because:

⚙ It is considered in email language that you are shouting.

⚙ It is uncomfortable on the eye.

⚙ It makes emails huge.

⚙ It makes it look as though you have an ego the size of a bus.

Recap: Key things to remember for your CV

⚙ Keep it to two pages.

⚙ Keep it concise.

⚙ Don't bother with writing the obvious just to fill up space.

Check List Chart for the Ultimate CV

Day 1

⚙ Photocopy your Certificates several times each.

⚙ Make up a file containing your Qualification and Product Training Certificates.

⚙ Get a good photograph.

⚙ Make a list of your qualifications.

Day 2

⚙ Make a note of your college and qualifications and dates of start and finishing the college.

⚙ Make a list of your jobs with dates, including months.

✪ Make a list of reasons for leaving those jobs.

✪ Get your references organized.

Day 3

✪ Make your CV.

✪ Make several copies of your CV and put it in your hard backed file.

Put a copy of your CV on to disk/CD/Flash Drive and store in your hard backed file. Store a copy in "Word" on your computer ready to email. Word is the most commonly used word processing software and so is easily downloaded by people you are sending your CV to.

You want to make it as easy as possible for people to find your file when you phone up to follow-up your phone calls later on, and you want them to save your file to your name so that your CV does not get lost on their computer under all the miscellaneous files called CV.

Naming your CV/File on your computer

Remember the file name you give your CV will be emailed to potential employers and Agencies; just calling it CV is only helpful to you and not the agency that has just received 4000 CVs that week! Ideally your CV document should be saved as "your name cv" and then the last two digits of the year. ie: NicoleBeecherCV10.

When you update your CV always ensure the file is dated in the correct year.

Check List

Curriculum Vitae
Your Name

Name
Address
Personal Details   Photo
D.O.B
Driver
Smoker/Non Smoker

Profile

> *A few lines about yourself and what you are looking for, framed in a box, to make it stand out. This paragraph about yourself can make the difference between someone reading your CV or not. It can make the difference between someone asking you for an interview or not. Spend time on really keeping your words succinct, concise and spelt correctly.*

Beauty Qualifications
Put in here your beauty college details.
Your start and finish dates of college.
Your qualifications gained.

Product Training and Additional Training
List here any product training including dates.

Career Details
Put in here your jobs, dates and role.
If you had part-time jobs whilst at college, make it clear.

Hobbies:
Hobbies do count, take them seriously. Someone who writes that their hobby is Drinking, Socialising, and Clubbing would set alarm bells ringing.

References: Consider carefully who you put forward.

- Save your file in Word Format.
- Name your File appropriately and with the correct date.
- Save your file and store a hard copy.

Having prepared your CV and now hopefully having a clear idea of what you want to achieve, you now need to decide how you are going to go about applying for jobs.

5

Finding Your Job

Getting the best out of your Agencies & Job Boards

There are Beauty Agencies, Job Boards, Direct Advertisements on the Internet and in Beauty Magazines, Business's Web Sites and Word of Mouth, Knocking on Doors, all methods of finding your job.

Now is a good time to consider the suitability of each method for you.

At various stages of your career, different methods will be more suitable. Sometimes discretion is required and sometimes it is not important.

At times you may benefit from having support, advice and help with salary negotiations, and that you would get from an Agency. They can act as a good buffer between you and your potential new employer. It is equally important for an Agency to make sure you get the right job as it is for their client to find the right employee.

With a Job Board you will be able to apply directly and to many companies very quickly. With an Agency it may take longer, but it may be more precise in finding the job that is most suitable for you at a salary that is negotiated. With the Job Board option you may find there are more jobs being advertised because not all salons can, or want to, afford the use of an Agency. You will find that some of the better jobs are with agencies, this indicates the salon is prepared to pay a fee for the right person and they take their staff recruitment seriously, and either want to get exactly the right person or do not have the time to go through lots of CVs. More often than not they will have a trusted Agency that knows the type of person they like and the standard they require and will recommend a few selected therapists that they know their client will like.

Magazines should not be ignored and are a good source of information in general, as well as for keeping up to date with the jobs market. Two that have been around for years and have a good following are *Professional Beauty* and *Health and Beauty Salon Magazine*. Other good publications to look at are Vitality from BABTAC and International Therapist from the FHT, European Spa Magazine, Scratch, Guild News and The Salon Magazine.

Beauty Recruitment Agencies

What are Beauty Recruitment Agencies?

Agencies find you work, and they find staff for the salons, spas, and clinics.

This can be full time, part time or temporary work. Their clients are the salons and it is their clients who pay them, to find the best staff.

Agencies in the beauty industry are not to be confused with a "modelling agency". A modelling agency may be concerned with your promotion, publicity, and taking over control of your career and signing you up as one of their "stars".

Beauty Agencies are there to introduce staff to employers and they guide, support and negotiate between the two parties. They are keen to ensure that they find you the perfect job and the salon the perfect therapist.

Agencies will work as a buffer between you and potential employers, smoothing the way, protecting you from dealing directly in the early stages and generally guiding you along. They will be recommending jobs, suggesting jobs, applying for the jobs, arranging the interviews, advising you on your interview details, assisting with your CV, helping negotiate the salary and commission and ensuring that you have the best offer available for that role. They will offer support and advice and often they will ensure that you get an interview that you might have had trouble securing if they were not introducing you to their client.

The Traditional Beauty Recruitment Agency

This agency will have relationships with the salons and spas and be actively searching and matching staff to jobs. They will want to ensure that you are right for the job and the job is right for you. They will only get paid for their work if they place you in the right job and you stay there. They will offer advice and support to both you and their clients, the salons, and they will set up your interviews and negotiate salaries for you. They will have a good idea if your expectations are realistic and they will advise accordingly. These agencies are safer if you need to keep your job search discreet because they will protect your identity. They are more suitable if you are making a career move and are at a stage in your career when you need to make sure the next job is right for you. You will find traditional agencies have web sites and you can register on line and on the phone.

Getting the best out of your traditional agency

When dealing with traditional agencies, remember they match jobs according to your requirements, so try to give them as much information as possible and if you have any concerns, discuss it with them, they will help you. Traditional agencies tend to be better for the more quality positions. If you are therefore putting yourself in that category then remember the agency will be looking for you to prove that you are a therapist who has the same standards as their clients. Their clients are paying them to find the best.

Avoid agencies that don't really listen to your requirements, that don't take the time to really understand what you want to achieve. A good one will listen and offer advice; even if it is not the advice you want to hear.

A good agency will not send out your CV to anyone without checking and discussing the job with you first. It is worth checking the agencies, policy on this point as it will prevent your CV going out to unsuitable jobs and getting your name around all over the place, making it look as if you are desperate. Also make sure that you know which jobs you have applied for because you do not want multiple agencies or job boards applying for the same job for you. There are further explanations and examples of why not later on in this chapter.

Ensuring your CV is not sent out without your knowledge may strike you as strange, given that in the next section I have written about Job Board/Listing Agencies who are sending out your CV anyway, but the two types of agencies are quite different in their approach.

Generally it is accepted that therapists going for the premium positions, and who are taking care to market themselves to match that level, are going to be using the traditional agency route and will take the time to discuss and control their job search. Those therapists will be the ones who want to maximise their potential, salary and prospects.

Good traditional agencies will speak with you about the position and then if you agree they will apply for the position for you. They will then set up the interview for you. It is in both your interests for you to give them your feed back on the position and then they will negotiate on your behalf with the salon for the salary package.

You will find that traditional agencies have web sites and have many of their positions on the sites for you to keep an eye on the market place.

Benefits of an Agency

- ⚙ They can often negotiate a higher salary than you would yourself.
- ⚙ Your agreed package is noted by them, useful sometimes if misunderstandings occur.
- ⚙ You will receive good advice and market information.
- ⚙ You'll get help with your CV and you'll be shown in your best light.
- ⚙ Your agency will often tip the balance between getting the job or not.
- ⚙ Companies will often ask an agency to keep a look out for positions that you won't see advertised.
- ⚙ Your agency will act as a buffer between you and the potential employer.
- ⚙ Your agency will shield you from embarrassing and difficult phone calls direct with the employer.

What to watch out for with an Agency

Leaving your number for them to ring and asking for a list of jobs as though it is your right is not going to get the best out of the more specialised agencies. You need to build a relationship and get to know them.

Remember an agency is a business and not a government service. A good agency also cares about their service to you and to their clients and they will respond to your needs if you respond to theirs. So remember that they have a choice between you and thousands of other therapists. If they feel that you are genuine and straight forward they are going to be more comfortable recommending you to their clients.

You need to be aware that if you are phoning lots of agencies there may be a conflict of interest in the jobs.

Most agencies will not have a problem with you signing up for several agencies.

It is helpful to make your Agency aware of other methods of job searching you are using so that they don't waste time on jobs you have already applied for. They will appreciate your honesty.

Zahra

Zahra phoned several agencies on the same day and inadvertently applied for the same job with all of them

Zahra asked for the advice of agency A, discussed her requirements with them and told them about her experience and qualifications. The agency suggested a job that would suit her, which was Management; a position she was enthusiastic about. Zahra agreed it sounded good, and she asked if they would apply for the position for her with their client.

Her Agency felt she was genuinely interested, she had impressed them, and so convinced were they that she was suitable for short listing that they approached the company in question to arrange an interview.

Based on their trust and past experience with the agency in question, the company agreed they would like to meet with Zahra and asked if she could attend the interview in two days' time. Zahra's agency left a message on her phone asking her to call to agree a convenient time for the interview. Zahra did not respond until the following day. She said she could not attend an interview the following day because she was working.

In fact, she was not working, she had arranged to go for another interview set up by another agency and for some reason she did not explain this; unfortunately the interview was with the same company that the first agency was waiting for her to confirm about!

To further complicate things, yet a third agency was also in the process of setting up an interview with the same company as well and, not only that, Zahra had applied for the same job directly with the same company on line. Zahra thought that by applying four times over she was assured of an interview and, determined to get the job, she thought this was the way to get noticed.

The result was that all the agencies were unhappy with Zahra and the potential employer was not impressed. They had received different versions of her CV from each agency and finally the one they received from Zahra – her own original one – was very out of date and badly prepared.

Even if the company had wanted to take Zahra on, which they absolutely did not, they would have had a predicament because they had inadvertently agreed with each of the agencies that they could set up an interview. This meant they would have had a problem with the fees, as all companies would claim the introduction fee.

By this time all parties were aware that this candidate was not showing any loyalty or understanding of the protocols of applying for jobs, was not showing herself in good moral standing, neither was she showing the Management skills which would be required for the position she wanted to obtain.

The interview went ahead but Zahra was turned down for it immediately.

Company B lost confidence in her, Company A didn't try any more because they believed she was working with another agency and she had lied to them about working when in fact she was going for an interview.

Company C didn't try for her anymore because when she spoke with them she had forgotten what she had said in her previous conversation. They had taken some time to help her decide the best career moves and they felt used.

Job Board Internet Sites – What are Job Boards or Listing Job Boards?

Think Monster, Fish, Gum Tree, Job Boards are purely a Listing Job Service. They send out lists or email alerts of jobs to you, and email alerts or lists of CVs to the employers advertising on their sites. They have advertisements on their site that you apply for directly to the employer. There is no go-between person on the telephone or personal relationship or talking involved and they do not get involved in the support or negotiation. Their service is to send you lists of jobs every day or week and you apply to those jobs directly. Job Boards are very good for those who would prefer to negotiate their own salaries and those whose objective is not career critical, or perhaps for those who are in the country for a year or so and just need a job to earn money and are not focusing on the bigger picture. The other advertisements you will find on Job Boards are from traditional agencies. When you apply for these jobs you will be dealing through the agency.

Many Job Boards work efficiently but you do need to be careful as they sometimes attract some of the salons that traditional agencies would know to avoid and of course this also works the other way with regards to the therapists they attract.

The salons who sign up for Job Boards will similarly receive lists of prospective candidates and the salons may contact you directly from their lists. These Listing Job Boards earn their income from the salons who will pay them a weekly/monthly fee for advertising their jobs for a set period of time and to receive lists of the candidates looking for work.

This method of job search is good for instant action and speed and it will also open up jobs for you that may not be available with Agencies. It is a cheaper method of advertising for the employer and they have to do their own ground work in sifting through the CVs and making contact with you, the potential employee.

Don't be put off by not receiving responses from job applications you have sent off. Virtually everyone complains that they have been ignored or there is no response. They all say it makes them feel disillusioned but in fact this is to misunderstand the concept of Job Boards.

The Salons/Businesses advertising on the Job Boards will sometimes get hundreds of applicants. They receive by email long lists of people as well.

They will receive many applicants who just send off their CVs to loads of jobs without looking to see if the job is relevant. They will get Newly Qualified applying for Senior positions, a Plumber or Truck

Driver applying for fun or just because they have not looked at the job spec, or so that they can say they have tried for jobs at the job centre, "honest mate I've done my best!"

In fact there is a strange psychology to this, in that, as they receive the CVs they become impersonal and annoyed that people are sending through CVs that are not exactly right for the job and are less likely to email back to respond, one way or another.

The applicants, however, are thinking that they may as well try to apply, even if they don't have the experience asked for, or maybe they have NVQ Level II qualification and the job asks for NVQ Level III, because you never know, they might just land a great job. Since they don't generally get a response anyway, they think they may as well apply.

The psychology behind the thinking would be correct from the applicant's point of view if they were at interview stage or were applying in the old ways, where the was a chance of a face-to-face meeting. However, with an application over the internet this thinking is no longer relevant.

Plus because of the enormity of the task for the employer who advertises on Job Boards to sift through to find the good CVs, your CV can get lost in the pile. This is another good reason to name your file (see Chapter 5).

What to watch out for

⊛ Watch out for your own information management skills when using this method.

⊛ Make a note to whom you speak and what you say.

⊛ If you are already working for someone, there is a good chance that they will also be looking for staff, and they may get your name on the list!

⊛ Think hard when signing up about your requirements and needs.

⊛ Be ready and prepared for your phone to ring at any time, with potential employers.

Remember your information will be being sent out to all and sundry or can be accessed by anyone who logs onto those sites, so what they see in writing is what they know about you; make it good because you don't have the support of an agency staff member watching out for you.

Be extra cautious, it is easier for the less desirable companies to employ staff through a Job Board. (Just as it is easier for the less desirable therapists to apply for jobs through this method.)

Your CV will be publicly on line for a long time.

Very Easy

Job Boards have become a very popular way for people to search for jobs and are convenient, so you can apply for jobs without picking up the phone or moving from your comfortable chair.

They can make it easy for you by emailing you new jobs that come on the books and will allow you to choose jobs by location, salary, or job title. They will give you the option of adding to your CV or typing one in and applying immediately for a job.

The very ease with which you can apply means you are quite likely to get carried away and apply for a number of jobs, and also to be a little bit casual with your presentation.

There are two fundamental mistakes that people make after applying on line for jobs on Job Boards.

The first is, they forget when they are sitting at their computer, quiet, efficient and organized and putting in their mobile phone number as a contact number to ring, that when the person phones back they will probably be in a different place, different mood, maybe travelling, or at a party or maybe they will be expecting a friend to ring and be putting on a silly voice or worse!

The second mistake is that many people have no idea how many jobs they have applied for and they have no idea what the jobs are or where they are located.

This is a problem because the expectant and hopeful advertiser who is probably sitting somewhere quietly with your CV in hand, their mind focused on your call and their job, is going to phone you expecting you to know immediately who they are and assuming you will be delighted to get the call.

They are then disappointed when they get some wild mad person on the end of the phone who clearly does not have a clue who they are and who clumsily tries to find out which job it is they are calling about.

With egos firmly dented, the telephone conversation is much harder than it need be. In the days when you had to apply by letter written by hand and a telephone call you would probably have thought much harder about the image you were presenting.

The nature of these Job Boards means that the person receiving your application may also be receiving very large numbers of responses from other people and will probably also receive a number of applications that are of no relevance to the job and from people who probably live out of the area anyway.

On the other hand, candidates looking for jobs have all said the same thing about Job Boards, for a large number of jobs they get no reply at all and they find it rude. Having this understanding of the cause and effect will mean you don't take it personally or become despondent if you don't get a reply.

Many Companies seeking the staff complain they find it hard work sifting through numerous CVs of people replying to their adverts who are not in any way suitable for the position. Despite the negatives, it is possible to get good jobs from these Job Boards but it is better to take care with your application.

Having looked at hundreds of CVs from these Job Boards, there is always a gem hidden somewhere and so you need to make sure you are that gem shining out from the pile of CVs in front of them. Also remember that you may go on several sites and you can make yourself look a little desperate if everyone has your CV. This is even more of a problem if you don't have the same version of your CV on each site.

Getting the best out of your Job Board:

Have your regular CV prepared and ready to load onto the Job Board upload section.

Make sure your CV is tidy, accurate, finished, professional and easy to read, ensuring you have the maximum chance of yours being read from the hundreds the person is going to receive.

It is not a good idea to try to type all your information into the email that is going to the advertiser, because when they receive it they will find it difficult to read. Make a short concise summary, with a good impact statement and refer to the job in question; they may be advertising several jobs.

Make sure you put your name, location and telephone number on the email summary statement.

They may not be able to open your CV and without the number being obvious they may not phone you.

Make a note of each job you apply for and ideally print off the copy of the advert.

Check that the job is in the right location for you and that it is the right type of job for your requirements before you apply.

Don't waste your time, or the employer's time applying for jobs that are totally out of your reach by location or job type.

Be prepared to receive a phone call at any time. How you answer that phone will make the difference. Whilst an agency may give you a little bit of time to recover yourself, a company will have already formed an opinion by the time you have pulled yourself together. Unfair as it may seem, if you answer unprofessionally, even though it's your private phone, the image you portray will lose you the job.

That is the downside of mobiles and the way we apply for jobs today.

Which Job Boards?

In order to put all of your energies into the right job applications it is better to focus on the Job Boards or Agencies that work for you.

There are many big names out there with some of the big generic Job Boards covering all types of jobs and industries who have a lot of advertising power on the television and in the press. It is not to say that you will not get the perfect jobs from these sites but if you prefer to condense your efforts into a few quality applications that you can control and monitor, then it is clearly better to work with the specialised sites relative to the beauty industry first and foremost, before going on to the generic ones.

That is not to say that the generic Job Boards should be dismissed because there is often a gem of a job that has been put on that might be missed by thousands of other therapists who are looking at the other sites.

With so many choices it is difficult to know which ones to choose and it is not a good idea to go on to too many. One simple way to reduce the choices when choosing which Job Board to use is to go for the specific industry-related web sites rather than the sites that cover all industries and all job types from Truck Drivers to Zoo Keepers.

Health and Beauty and *Professional Beauty* magazines have both very good Job Boards. They have both been in the beauty industry for many years and have experience in the Beauty Market and a loyal following in the industry. See www.professionalbeautyjobs.co.uk and www. hji.co.uk

A fairly new job board, Topjobs4leisure, is also a good one to consider. They are smaller and offer a more personal service than other Job Boards. They have a very user friendly site and whilst they cover several sectors of the leisure industry they are very focused on the beauty side. The owner has a Beauty Industry background and takes a personal interest in your success. www.topjobs4leisure.com.

Which Agencies?

Again, as with Job Boards, it is better to go for an Agency that is dedicated specifically to the Beauty Industry.

Choosing which Agency is better for you will be predominantly a matter of personality, whom you feel you get on with, who has the better jobs suited to your requirements, and whom you feel will do the best job for you.

Because you are not the one who is paying their fees, you do not have to be directly concerned about their charges. Although indirectly their fees do effect you; the higher salary they achieve in negotiations for you, the higher the fee they charge the salon within certain salary brackets.

They want to get the best person for the job for their client and they want that person to stay in the job, so they want both their client and the candidate to be very happy with the introduction. Both parties could be potential clients again and the job satisfaction for an agency is in a successful match.

Most agencies work on results, so they do all of their work for their client upfront; this will include the time they spend on support, advice, and the advertising overheads they incur to bring you to their agency. They then have to decide whether you are the person that is right for the job out of lots of other candidates.

If you are offered the job, and you accept and start, then they get paid.

Most agencies will cover the whole of the UK and some have work abroad as well.

Agencies will offer you advice, support and will introduce you to jobs that you may not otherwise find. They will open doors for you to clients who may not want to use the job boards, or who may want discretion, to clients who prefer the expertise of the agency, or who simply do not have the time to go through lots of CVs and interviews. Agencies will short list people who fit the client's brief exactly and therefore the salon owner does not have to waste valuable time on reading CVs and interviewing people who are not suitable. Agencies will hand hold your job search and prep you before your interview, assist with your CV, assist with finding you a job that meets your criteria and negotiate with the salon on your behalf, ensuring that all parties are happy and understand the employment terms before you start.

You will find Agencies advertising in Beauty Magazines and on the Internet. They will be advertising their jobs on the Job Boards and by word of mouth. Many of the jobs you see on Job Boards and Newspapers will have been placed by Agencies.

Beauty Recruitment Plus can be found on
www. beautyrecruitment.com
Tel: 01483 451432.
Email: info@beautyrecruitment.com
Beauty Specialists in the Beauty Industry covering London and Nationwide.

For Hair and Beauty try
www.rosemariehadley. com.
Tel: 0207 584 1990
Email: rose@rosemariehadley.com
Specialists in Hair and Beauty and Temping covering London.

Beauty Consultants Bureau
www.bcb.uk.com
Tel: 0207 287 8060
Specialists in Temporary Sales and Promotional Consultants London and Nationwide.

Mixing Methods of Job Search – In the example that follows, the candidate was using various methods for her job search

The candidate was put forward for a job by an agency, the salon said they had already received the CV. They said that they had dismissed it because they had received it from other Job Boards for several months and they felt that there must be something wrong with her if she had been on so many sites for such a long time.

In fact the agency felt she was very good but they were not now in a position to represent the candidate, as she had in effect gone directly to the company, thus the company would not pay an agency fee.

Unfortunately for the candidate, the Agency then decided that they too would not try too hard for her because she was sending her CV to everyone so they would encounter the same problem whoever they tried to introduce her to.

You may think, so what? Well the problem here is that she kind of saturated her own market. Had she made herself a little more exclusive with any one of the methods of job search, she would have been able to achieve a better and higher paid job than she did, but collectively she watered down the effect of each of the methods that she used.

One Therapist who nearly came a cropper with both Agency types in one go!

A Therapist who used both methods of Agency was completely unaware of the consequences of the actions she was taking and the possible effects on her plans.

Having decided she needed a new job she joined a Job Board, giving her potential job requirements as

£14K to £15K salary, no Saturdays and no late shifts and London only. This Therapist was not very good at promoting herself in her own best light and in fact was quite self-deprecating. Although competent in her treatments she did not inspire confidence in her ability.

A month or so after joining the Job Board, the Therapist reviewed her situation and realised the listing agency had provided, exactly as promised, lists of jobs.

She had also been contacted by salons who had her name on their lists from the Listing Agency, but, she had not had any interviews.

At this point she contacted a Traditional Agency, one that had in fact got her her first ever job in the industry when she left college, and this agency remembered her, knew of her background and the salon she had worked for. Luckily when she phoned she got right through to the original consultant that had placed her in her first job and who remembered her straight away.

The Traditional Agency, with the benefit of knowing her, put forward a suggestion of a job they were working on. They got her to check out the journey and spent some time discussing the position with her; establishing what her career goals were and explaining the job content to ensure it was the right job for her. They discussed the salary expectations of both her and the salon owner. The Therapist advised the Traditional Agency that she wanted a minimum of £17K and her main objective was to find a job in a particular part of London to enable her to move in with a friend.

The Traditional Agency set up the interview with the salon, sending them her CV and discussing her background with them. The salon had wanted to find someone at around £15 to £16k per annum maximum. The agency advised the salon that this candidate was looking for around the £16K to £17K mark.

There were various hurdles along the way that could have thwarted the candidate's prospects. Because of the Agency's past history with the candidate, the Agency was able to show the candidate in her best light, explaining that whilst she was quite a quiet person, she did make clients feel that she was calm and strong and peaceful.

The first interview was cancelled due to the candidate having an accident and the salon began to get cold feet. The salon was concerned and thought they should forget the interview. The Agency, knowing this was a genuine reason for not attending, managed to restore this situation and rebook the interview for a better time, allowing some extra time for the therapist to sort out some other problems.

The night before the re-booked interview, the salon telephoned the Agency to say they were just reading her CV and that somewhere in their memory they were sure they had spoken with this candidate before on the phone, and, furthermore if it was the same girl, when they had spoken with her she had said that she did not want a job that included Saturdays or weekends and, worse than that, on the list provided by the Listing Agency, she had said she wanted a salary of £14K to £15K.

Naturally, the salon did not want to waste valuable time on an interview if the candidate was going to say at the end that she did not want Saturdays or evenings. The Agency was left with the problem that they needed recover the negative feelings the salon had towards the candidate. Once that was overcome they would need to get the candidate the salary she wanted, however with the handicap that she had inadvertently told the salon she would accept a lower salary.

The Agency also had the problem that the salon was already concerned because of the previous cancelled interviews and a telephone call that had not impressed them very much.

The Traditional Agency contacted the Therapist who did not remember this telephone conversation with the salon. She then explained that she had previously gone to a Listing Job Board and on receipt of a list of jobs had phoned them all up, not really focusing on what she was saying.

She had not realised that this interview was one of the companies she had rung up, and furthermore she had not told the Traditional Agency that she had given the Listing Agency a different criteria. This was not deliberate; she just had not put the two together in her mind as being important.

Unfortunately she had not made a good impression on the telephone when she spoke with the salon originally. Neither had she made a note of the salons she had rung or what she had said to them. Lastly, she had mentioned a different salary expectation than the one she had given the Traditional Agency.

The Traditional Agency did manage to convince the salon that the Therapist was happy to work Saturdays and two evenings a week and a salary was negotiated that suited both parties. The match was made and everyone was happy. But she was lucky. With such an unprofessional approach to her application she might have lost the job. Without the agency to rescue the situation, she certainly would have done.

6

Job Application Clangers

Inefficiency or efficiency or just plain can't be bothered?

The Round Robin

Sending multiple agencies and salons round robin emails and letters is a social blunder and will hinder your job search.

To an agency that cares about getting you the right job, at the right salary, this will be offensive. It will say to them that either this person does not understand what an agency does and is confusing them with a Job Board, or that this person can't be bothered, is a waste of time, is not professional and, significantly, all the other agencies are going to have her on their books. Therefore the conclusion is that there is no point in spending any time on her because she will probably be gone soon anyway.

To both salons and agencies it will say that clearly she does not understand business discretion or tact, indicating a possible problem with passing on information with competitors if discussing a potential job.

To a salon it indicates that you are struggling to get a job and don't know how to be discreet because you have just put everybody's email addresses in your contact list and they may not want to be there. Or perhaps you are claiming benefit, need to prove that you have contacted lots of people for work, and this way can say you wrote to twenty people this week. The conclusion being, therefore, that you are not really interested in getting a job and that's why you have been so careless – because you don't care.

Whoa! … You, however, thought you were being efficient, impressing them with your email skills. It may well work because you get to a lot of people quickly, and you can say to your parents/spouse or school that you are being pro-active.

You will probably not know which Agency or Salon they are when they phone you up. You will probably have left your mobile number for them to ring. The Agency or Salon will be thinking that here they are spending money on an expensive mobile call when it is obvious you do not have a clue who they are. Of course they will think that you have probably been contacted by all the other people in the round robin email and therefore they are better off using their time on all the other CVs they have yet to get through.

You don't have their number to call them back and it's highly probable that you will receive the call when you are on the bus, in a shop, in a coffee shop, and are not in a position to write it down, and unfortunately their number did not come up on your mobile.

The Agency may try to call you back but the position is not now to your advantage. Remember if they call you back they are expecting you to be able to speak about the type of job you are looking for. Any Agency worth their salt will be very keen to get you the best job, at the best salary; they will have an equal loyalty to you as they will have to their client.

Just because an Agency phones you to discuss a position does not mean the job is yours. I have had countless therapists tell me that they have just been offered a job in xyz, in fact they have not, they have just been informed about it. So the message here is, don't turn down further opportunities for job interviews because you think you have been offered a job, when in fact all you have been offered is a conversation about a job.

Mobile phone clangers

The mobile phone phenomenon has revolutionised the job search for Beauty Therapists. The anomaly here though is that many college leavers have entered the employment world only ever knowing the world as one on the end of a mobile, many people in the business world have only grudgingly come to accept it as part of today's society.

Agencies have now come to accept that 70% of their phone bill is going to be due to calling mobiles.

However, that does not change the fact that they are more than aware that when you ask them to call you back it is costing them a lot of money.

Having this facility has undoubtedly helped therapists in their job search in that they are able to take their own messages privately, without family members getting involved. The therapist has the option of checking the messages and making calls in lunch hours, thus obviating the long wait for the result of a job interview until getting home, or being able to respond quickly to the opportunity of an interview when an agency or business leaves a message.

The down side is, and this is a big one, to many therapists their mobile phone is their lifeline to their social life and friends. It is their own piece of independence, their own piece of personal identification, their own stamp on individualisation, which is great in your social world, but can be detrimental to your career.

Scenario 1

Imagine if you will, you have a day off, the house to yourself, your computer is working and the internet ready to roll; better than that you are in the right mood, positive, ambitious, determined and confident that you are going to rock the world so you apply for jobs, do your CV, apply to agencies, your efficient and capable self comes across confident, bubbly and knowing what you want in life. You send out all your messages, completing registration forms for jobs etc. The next morning you are fast asleep in bed and your mobile rings, you answer, it is probably your best buddy to talk about last night, you answer yer, umm, yer who is it. Oh yer umm.

You have just lost the job.

Scenario 2

You have just had the same productive day and applied to loads of agencies. Someone helped you with your CV and it looks fantastic, the Agency has a mental image of this professional go-getter who is undoubtedly a high-calibre candidate and clearly a therapist who will be suitable for the best jobs at the highest salary. Exactly what the most desirable company would be looking for.

Three days later you receive a call, you are in a bar with friends having a laugh. You answer the call laughing and say you have not got time to talk at the moment. You are sounding not interested and eating a bag of crisps, then your ego takes over because all your friends are listening and you have had a glass of wine, you tell (you don't even ask) the agency to call you back. If you are lucky the agency or company may just call you back, unfortunately they then get your answer service which you have put on a catchy tune so they have to listen to it for three minutes whilst paying a mobile phone charge.

You have not only just lost the job but you have also completely blown the image your professional self wanted to convey and the person probably thinks you are not serious about your job search and in fact are probably a time-waster.

The fact is we all have different sides to our personalities when we are at home, in work, with our friends and with our partners. Those therapists that have grown up in the mobile world should understand that for the business world, the casualness of the way the mobile phone is answered can be damaging for the therapist, sales person, receptionist, business or anyone at all.

Imagine if you have applied for a Reception position and you answer the call badly. The person at the other end will know that you cannot be relied upon to answer their business phone call automatically well. How can they then put you in charge of their business line?

The bottom line here is, if you are going to hand out your mobile phone for business replies then answer it properly at all times or turn it off, or get a separate mobile phone for job searching.

Key mistakes to avoid when searching for a job

Don't ring from work in your employer's time: people make a note of these things. It's unprofessional and it is an abuse of their time and money.

Don't put silly messages on your mobile phone – if you want to impress. You can always change it back when you are no longer searching.

Don't put on long music tracks that answer your phone. Business people do not have the time or the inclination to listen for three minutes to your music whilst they wait to leave a message for you.

Don't assume that it is your right to ask people to ring an expensive mobile phone.

Other people's experiences – The Tale of Hapless Hepi

This is a good example of a classic mistake that people make time and time again.

Hapless Hepi contacted an Agency through their web site. Hapless Hepi could have been one of a thousand therapists coming on the books that week. Hapless Hepi had already made at least five mistakes before she even had a conversation with the Agency. She had registered on line but only half filled in the form, she had not sent in her CV as requested. When the Consultant at the Agency called her, Hepi could not even manage to say hello, the Consultant enquired "are you there?" Hepi was unable or unwilling to say yes or no, she just grunted. Asked again, she grunted once more. The Consultant could not understand if she was saying 'yes'; or 'no' or if she had a speech impediment or maybe she could not speak English. The Consultant, at a loss to know if this was Hepi or not, said "I guess that's a 'no'? Miraculously Hepi then summoned up the strength to say 'this is Hepi and I am sorry but I am fast asleep, may I call you back in half an hour.' Of course the answer was yes.

When Hepi did phone back the Consultant did not recognise her, here was a bright and bubbly person to whom they gave the benefit of earlier doubt, and opened up the discussion of the type of job that she was looking for. It turned out that Hepi had been qualified for six months and had not had a job in the industry and so would be classed as newly qualified. The Consultant asked her what sort of environment she would ideally like to work in and the only answer Hepi could give was that she wanted a company that would give her training. She didn't want a company that just gave her a book to read and get on with it. Then she went on for a good ten minutes saying what else she didn't want, going on and on about companies that didn't give training, and then she continued to moan about bad salon owners.

This is what her conversation was conveying with her tone and words.

I don't care about the job environment, I want money and training.

I am not interested in offering anything to the salon.

I want what I can get out of the salon.

I want my rights.

The salon owner is the enemy and I know all about that.

I have worked for some dodgy salons.

In fact the experienced Consultant was fully aware that this was not what Hepi was really trying to say or imply and that Hepi simply did not realise how her words could impact on potential employers. The Consulant knew that it was due to her lack of experience that was coming across in this way. The Consultant knew that she would have to gently guide Hapless Hepi so that she would not be misunderstood by a potential employer.

Without any experience of her own, Hepi had been told by her friends who already had jobs about their experiences and, nervous of picking the wrong job, she was using this information from her friends to define the role that she wanted and it was coming across as very negative.

This is an important point to remember – your experience in the same salon with the same boss can be completely different to another person's; it is how you handle yourself, the job or the task that dictates your experience.

Just because her friends had worked for salons and obviously had negative experiences, she was using their version of events to define her job search and was coming across with a certain attitude. She was assuming that the experience of her friends was all there was out there.

When you are looking for a position, have a list in your mind of the criteria you want, and this comes back to your preparation in Chapter 2. You will keep in mind that you are looking for a job with location/training/salary/etc. You will then, when you apply for a job, remember that it is a two-way thing; they want to know what you can bring to the table as well.

Your Email Address

Make sure the email address you use for your job applications is ideally your name or something that looks very professional.

Just as we all form opinions within the first few seconds of meeting someone, based on their visual appearance, so too with your email address.

This is particularly important if you are applying for jobs via Job Boards or by yourself. (An Agency does not show your email address to the salon.)

Otherwise, you will be turned down for jobs and you will not be aware of the reason why.

An example of an email address that would not be suitable is :

Vodkapartygirl@xyz
Crazyclubber@xyz

You could always have an email address just for professional purposes and another for your friends.

7

Interviews and Trade Tests

Now you have successfully secured yourself an interview, it is preferable to give yourself a little time to prepare. If you have an Agency working for you, they will be the buffer between you and the Salon, so you will be able to check your diary for good dates and times without being flustered. A good Agency will be happy to work with you on this, knowing that you will be better prepared. If they feel that you need nudging towards a particular day they will tell you this as well. They will also advise you on the interview arrangements, and find out for you what will be expected of you at the interview.

If you have set up the interviews directly from Job Boards then you will not have the buffer of your agent and may receive a phone call at an inconvenient moment, when you may be so flustered that you can't think straight. A good plan is to create your own buffer by agreeing to the interview, asking the person on the end of the phone if you could check your diary/rota dates etc, and call them back to confirm. This way you can make sure you are not double booking and you will have time to get your pen and paper to take all the details. Or ask them to email them to you.

Before your interview, whatever level of experience you have and whatever method of job search you have used, you should do some planning. The three things you must do are:

✓ Research the Company;

✓ Plan what to wear;

✓ Check out the journey.

Research

Do some research on the company that is interviewing you.

This is well worth the effort, whatever level of experience you have. Do some background home-work on the company you are going to see.

If the company has a website then you can get a really good idea about who they are, what they stand for, treatments they do, products they use and the image they like to portray.

There are other considerations when doing the research that may help you decide, for example, on what to wear for the interview, and what sort of make up will suit the company. Some environments, such as Department stores, prefer a made-up look and some companies a fresh-faced look.

Lucky Lucy

Lucy had passed her first interview with an Aromatherapy company and she really wanted the job.

Her second interview was going to involve meeting the Managing Director. Lucy came from a Department store background in which it was normal to be fully made up. The Manager, who interviewed her, liked her very much but was not sure that she would pass the second interview with the Managing Director.

Luckily the Manager of the company was an experienced Manager, knew the value of a quiet word in the right ear and diplomatically and privately told the Agency that the candidate was ideal for the job but she would need to adopt a more natural look in order to fit in with the ethos of the company, to ensure that the busy Managing Director concentrated on her perfect CV rather than her look, at the second stage interview. The agency managed to diplomatically advise the candidate and the job was offered and everybody was happy.

Doing your home work on the company will ensure that when you go for your interview you will be informed about the company, their products, their ethos and their philosophy and they will be pleased that you have shown the initiative to learn about them.

Trade Tests

Sweaty Betty

Most salons will ask you to perform a trade test and this is often a few shortened treatments, but can be full-length ones.

A typical trade test, for example, could be a bikini wax, manicure, back massage, mini facial, a little bit of electrolysis and often an eyelash tint. The person trade testing you will be looking for all sorts of clues as to your attention to detail and customer care skills, not withstanding your ability to perform the treatments.

If this is your first interview and you are straight from college then the salon will more than likely be aware of your inexperience and will often be forgiving on mistakes if they think you have the ability to learn or if perhaps it is just nerves getting in the way.

It is often the little things that can lose you the job and this can happen at any level of experience due to lack of confidence, your mind on other things, sheer carelessness or being too casual or even over-confident.

I once sent a therapist for an interview who had six years' experience, was very precise about the type of salon she wanted to work for and had been strongly criticising her current company for its lack of hygiene, citing this as one of the reasons she wanted to get a new job.

Sweaty Betty got lost going to the interview and arrived flustered. She recovered once she was in the interview and then was asked to perform a hand massage.

At this point she should have asked if she could go and change into her uniform and then she could have taken a moment to wash her hands and compose herself.

What she in fact did was to say "okay, I suffer from very sweaty hands" and proceeded to perform this massage. I can only imagine the reaction of a less than delighted interviewer!

Yuk! Who wants sweaty hands touching them anywhere. Apart from this obvious error, she made quite a few fundamental mistakes with this interview and here was someone who had six years' experience!

Generally you will find that salons look for different things in their therapists. It might be that they need you to have a strong hand with massage, or that you specialise in electrolysis, or they may want people that excel with advanced waxing and in addition are also good general all-rounders.

If you are going through an agency, your agency will normally know if the salon is looking for specific skills and will probably have picked you because they know that your forte matches that of the salon, but if you are going it alone then it is a good idea to ask the salon if they have any particular treatments for which they get a lot of bookings, or if there is any area in which they specialise.

The salon will have no hesitation in asking you if you have any strengths or weaknesses with treatments at the interview and will deem it a sensible question for you to ask them. There is nothing wrong with saying that you are not so strong on a particular treatment as long as you follow it up with what you are good at and assess whether you are able to improve with practice or if you think you will genuinely never be any good at that treatment.

Checking out the journey first

What Sweaty Betty in the previous paragraph could also have done is to check out the journey sometime before the interview day. Instead she left it until the day of the interview, and it was in a place she had never been to before, so it was bound to be stressful.

In fact, I had actually said to her the week before that she should go there on the Sunday before with her husband to check it out, knowing that she was unfamiliar with the area.

If you get so stressed with worrying the night before about getting to the interview and then worrying on the day about finding it, and worrying all the way about getting there on time, by the time you arrive you have used up all your adrenalin and will have nothing left for the interview.

Presentation for your interview

Presentation is not just about getting the job, it tells the interviewer about your personality and standards.

Going to an interview with a stained old college uniform is just not going to cut the mustard. Your appearance is absolutely vital in this industry and you may hear people saying that it is your personality that counts or your fabulous skills as a therapist, but that is just not the case. This industry is all about how we and our clients look and feel. Your client wants to know that the therapist working on her or him is clean and has impeccable standards; the client may want to seek your advice on which products to use, which make up to wear and which treatments to have. How can they do that if they feel that the person working on them is grubby and clearly not someone to aspire to be!

An experienced therapist who had worked in some of the most fantastic and exclusive spas in London said to me that she makes sure that she looks amazing every day. Her appearance is very important to her and when she is getting ready every morning she reminds herself that she wants her clients, that day, to want to be like her, to aspire to look as good as she does, ask her opinion and advice. She wants them to notice her, respect her for her high standards, ask for her advice and knowledge to help them improve themselves. She wants to feel that she has helped them to do just that.

The first impressions do count and when you walk into that interview the person you are meeting will be looking at your hair, nails, shoes, uniform, make-up, everything, and all this will be assessed before you have finished saying "hello".

It is amazing how many people say they don't have a uniform to wear to go to an interview. If you really cannot afford to buy one then you must make up an outfit that looks suitable for doing a trade test, and one that you can change into. I don't mean a pair of jeans and t shirt, perhaps a smart pair of black yoga pants and white shirt or something that looks neat, clean and allows you to move to perform treatments.

Neither is it a good idea to wear your uniform to the interview, it is better to take it to change into when you are asked to perform a trade test. Many salons will consider inappropriate to wear a uniform on the journey to the interview as it could get dirty.

It is a good idea to have a set of "interview clothes". This would ideally be a suit or something very smart to arrive in. You should have them always clean and ready to wear at a moment's notice.

If you really have no smart clothes to wear then it is better to wear a uniform to arrive in rather than something entirely inappropriate.

Remember your taste does not necessarily match the image of the company or the taste of the person interviewing you, and so clothes that make a statement are not always a good idea, unless the salon is one that is looking for a particular type to match the statement they are making.

I had a candidate once that I primed before her interview to go in smart interview clothes and I was astounded afterwards to find out that she wore a cropped top (bra less) and hipster trousers and her piece de resistance was her pierced and jewelled belly button.

The salon I had sent her to was a holistic and natural salon catering to all age groups of clientele. This was a very well-known company, nobody could have mistaken their business philosophy, absolutely no one would not have heard of them even in outer Mongolia!

I asked her what made her wear such an outfit and she said "well you asked me to wear my best clothes" and I realised at that point that we were poles apart in our two definitions of smart clothes for interview. Therefore, for the avoidance of any doubt whatso-ever, I implore you to wear a suit or the classic fail-safe smart black trousers and white blouse!

Attitude

Tetchy Tracey the Lecturer

You don't need to be inexperienced to make a mistake in an interview; some of the most seasoned therapists make big mistakes and one such person was actually a Lecturer in the industry with twenty years' experience behind her and with a confidence that comes with age! This means that those of us who have reached this particular standard in life can sometimes shoot ourselves in the foot!

This particular Lecturer went for an interview for a Training position with a product house. After the interview, the two people interviewing her were on the fence as to whether she would be suitable or not. They felt that she had the right qualifications, background and experience; however they were not 100% sure if she was right for the job and neither could put their finger on why they felt this way. They had several other candidates who they could choose from.

That evening, on the day of the interview in question, the principal Manager who had held the interview left work, stopping for a chat with the car park attendant of the company car park. They chatted about their day, swapping stories, and during this conversation it transpired that the car park attendant had had a rotten day and one of the things that contributed to this was an altercation with a lady who had been for a meeting at the company and had tried to park in the company car park, which was for staff only. He had politely said that she was not allowed to park there and showed her where she should go instead. The lady in question had been very abusive to him and said she had a disabled badge. He pointed out that it was not for her disability and that she could not park there.

The lady lost her temper with him and the end result was that he was very upset and it ruined his day.

The Manager listened to this story and realised that the person he was talking about was the very person she had interviewed and had been undecided about.

The company did not want someone with such a short fuse and if she was prepared to fib about the disability badge, what would she be like with the company? Needless to say Tetchy Tracey was turned down for the job, officially because she did not have the experience, in reality because of her attitude.

8

Particularly for the Newly Qualifieds

Choosing a Career Path

Planning Your Career for 10 years time!

Although we are not all able to think clearly about the path we wish to take in life, by choosing to become a beauty therapist you have at least given yourself a starting point from where you can guide your career forwards by choosing the most effective path to achieve your ultimate goal. The hardest part of this is being honest with yourself, uninfluenced by any emotions, so that you plan with a clear, calm head.

Deciding that you want to go and work abroad the morning after a row with the boyfriend and six Gin & Tonics, for example, is questionable.

Whatever your age at the time of qualifying and what ever your master plan for your career, it is recommended that you get a job in a salon environment for a minimum of a year when you leave college. Ideally make sure that this first position is in a suitable environment for a Newly Qualified Therapist.

The best job you can get when you are Newly Qualified is one in which the salon owners have the time and resources to offer you personal development and support, where they can offer training courses on their products and guidance with your new skills. They will be aware that you are newly qualified and that you will need support.

You may be offered positions that appear more glamorous, more lively, more trendy or for more money but for the serious professional I would ignore all of those things and seek out the salon owner who can dedicate time and effort to your development. This is going to be fundamental to your future.

Now you must reciprocate by being honest, conscientious and open to their criticism, for what they are offering you is a cost to themselves and a risk. The risk is that at the end of your first year you will be feeling confident and want to move on. This is their cost because the salon has then lost the benefit of time and energy invested in you. The salon's hope, of course, is that you will want to stay and they will then benefit from having a perfectly groomed therapist who is trained in their methods, and knows their clients. This is often where a salary increase is timely in order to encourage you not to look elsewhere. It is very good for your CV if you do remain in your job for longer and is often a way of moving up the ladder into Management, greater commissions on more expensive treatments and further training.

There are various directions that therapists want to move towards and many personal goals they can strive to achieve. You have the opportunity of directing your career towards your ultimate goal.

Your first job in the industry

That first job works almost like a finishing school and, however confident you feel, there are always going to be experiences in a salon that cannot be anticipated or re-created in a college class room. These experiences are to be welcomed and not feared as that is how you learn. You will learn new techniques from your boss and colleagues, product training and new treatments. You will learn from experiences with clients, you will speed up your treatments such as waxing, manicures, pedicures and the finishing touches will become more important to you. Once you have mastered remembering all of the core skills, you will be more relaxed and able to remember all the extras.

Some salons will have their own signature treatments and some salon owners like to make sure that all of their staff performs all of their treatments in exactly the same way. This is to ensure that the client receives the same treatment and same standard that they have come to expect from that salon.

Your first job in many ways is the most important job of your career and is all part of building yourself a solid foundation. I would generally advise finding a salon that will give you the opportunity to use all of your treatments and who has the ability to support, guide and train you further in your first vital year. If you have decided already that you do not want to go down the traditional salon path and that you would rather specialise in a particular area and are sure that you will never need your other skills then it may be okay for you to go down your specialisation path. Generally, though, I would suggest that you "future proof" yourself again by getting a firm grounding in all of your treatments before going off into different directions.

Not all salons have the man time to support you or even the knowledge and so this is a tricky time for you in terms of ensuring you pick the right job with the right employer. If you are lucky enough to find an employer that gives you this support and training they will also be giving you their time and the benefit of their experience, so be appreciative and recognise this effort.

Sadly for these salon owners, they are often the losers for being mentors means that more often than not the therapist that they have nurtured wants to leave after the first year, having found her feet in the industry and wanting to diversify or perhaps just wanting more money. It is therefore a good idea if you are enjoying working in that salon to have a chat with the owner and explain what is causing your itchy feet so that they have the opportunity to see if they can find a way to encourage you to stay.

Getting your Mum to phone!

This is not about having a go at parents, this is about you understanding that it is now up to you to take responsibility for yourself. When you leave college and start going for interviews, you are suddenly in control of your career. People interviewing you will be thinking of their business and are looking for someone who will contribute to their business. You will be in a situation where you are looked upon as an individual and an adult. The salons will take into account your lack of experience with treatments but they will not want to find that every time there is a problem at work your Mother or Father will be on the phone.

It is perfectly okay if your parents phone up agencies or prospective employers to ask for advice or information, or to get an application form on your behalf, or to do the initial research. However, the Agency or salon will still want to talk to you, to get to know you, because you will be the one they employ and work with and so you will have to phone them back anyway.

You would be surprised at how many salon and agency stories there are on this subject and so it would not be giving you all of the information required to get a job in the beauty industry if this was left out.

An Agency or Salon will have more confidence in you if you have spoken with them directly. It will avoid them having niggling doubts in the back of their mind when you arrive for interview.

If your Mum is phoning to get you interviews, the Salon or Agency may consider that there is a good chance that your Mother is probably concerned and you have not taken the initiative, are too scared or maybe you have just not made any effort, or maybe you are not interested, and so what does this say to an employer?

As luck would have it, or not!

A Newly Qualified's Mother phoned a recruitment company on behalf of her daughter to see if there were any positions available. As luck would have it, the Agency happened to have a very good job on the books at that moment, and had in fact been trying without success to reach her daughter. Therefore, it seemed opportune to discuss the position with her Mother and an interview was set up.

The Agency asked the Mother if she would check with her daughter before making the appointment and asked Mum if she would get her daughter to call the Agency back. Mum said "no, there was no need to speak with her daughter" and insisted that her daughter would attend the interview, come what may.

On the day of the interview the Newly Qualified Therapist did not show up. The Agency rang her and she said she could not go because she was already going on a training course and it was clear she had no interest or intention of going to the interview. The Agency had allowed themselves to be persuaded that it would be okay and of course were embarrassed that they had let their client down.

The reputation of the Therapist was permanently damaged with the Agency and the Company.

Why is that first job in a salon environment so important?

It is where you become confident, experienced and where your mistakes are corrected, where your rough edges are smoothed over. Later on in your career salons will always look at your CV of what your first job was as an indicator to see what your standards will be like. If you went straight to work for yourself from college they will flag up a concern.

All that Glitters is not Gold

This saying also applies later on in your career as an experienced therapist, when money is more the focus in your job search. It is often the case that as an experienced therapist you can earn more money in a regular salon than in a trendy glamorous place. The following example shows how Mary went wrong in succumbing to the allure of the glamorous salon.

Mary's Mistake

Mary's Mistake in this case was to fail to gain a firm foundation as a college leaver. Mary had a golden opportunity but could not see it and asked her Mother to phone a recommended agency to find her a job. The agency asked a few key questions to try to ascertain what exactly Mary was looking for; the College Mary was just about to leave normally had visits from spas and cruise ships offering jobs to the college leavers. Knowing this, the Agency thought this might Indicate that perhaps Mary was not keen on any of the offers normally available.

It appeared that Mary had already been offered a position in a local salon where she had worked part-time for two years whilst she was at college.

This was good news and significant because some experience in a salon, before leaving college would assist her candidate greatly with her job search.

Knowing how difficult it is for a Newly Qualified Therapist to find a position, the agency asked the obvious question "why does Mary want to look for another job when she has already secured a job offer?" Mum said "I want her to have experience in another salon, preferably in London."

It is always hard for Newly Qualified's to get a job in a good nurturing salon. When the country is in an economically challenging time, as was the case in this example, it is even harder and it is often the college leavers that find it the most difficult to find jobs.

Mary was in the enviable position of having a job offer with a company, so she already had a head start. There were thousands of Newly Qualified's emerging from colleges without jobs at this time and employers were not in positions to offer them jobs.

The Agency decided that the best advice they could give was to gently try to guide the Mum in the direction of encouraging Mary to take the job offer she already had.

The Agency pointed out that the existing job offer Mary had secured all by herself was a very good opportunity. The Mother said that well of course her daughter would be taking the position, but she wanted Mary to just take the job for now, while she looked for something else.

At this point the Agency felt sorry for both Mary and the salon who had offered her the job.

Mary would take the job, without any real commitment to the salon. She would not be taking the job with the right attitude, because she was only doing it as a stop-gap to something 'apparently' better. The salon would end up disappointed because the therapist would not be as enthusiastic as they had expected and they would soon begin to have doubts as to her commitment, then they would be reluctant to offer training and commitment themselves.

Mary was about to mess up a job that would have been a fantastic firm foundation for her career, which would benefit her for the rest of her life. Mary and her Mum needed to look past the apparent glamour and glitz of other salons and look at what the local salon was offering her. She had already been with them two years whilst at college and on joining them full time she would have received training, guidance, practice and confidence for the next two years at least, making her CV look fantastic for her first job.

An Agency will want to build a relationship, get to know you and understand what you really want. They will want to know if there are any underlying reasons for your decisions on your job search. They will help you overcome any objections or concerns. In this instance the agency felt reluctant to look for a job for this candidate for so many reasons and some of those reasons Mary could probably have overcome if she had phoned herself. But they had only spoken with her Mother. The CV had been emailed by her Mother and the normal questions that would have been asked just to build rapport were not available.

Shocked Sarah

Mistakes do happen, it's how they are dealt with that counts

We have all heard the jokes about waxing mistakes, but this really did happen.

Imagine how Sarah felt when she took off a client's complete eyebrow by accident. The fear, shock and horror of what she had done could clearly be seen on her face by the client, who then went into panic and screamed "what have you done to me"? Sarah ran out of the room to get help, she had no idea what to say or do. Then, the relief of support as her capable and trusty Manager took control of the situation, calmed the client down, all the time reassuring the client, whilst gently manouvering the now "in bits" Sarah out of the room, and not allowing herself to show any fear; the Manager inspected the offending eyebrow and reassured the client that not all of the eyebrow had been removed, it would just need a little re-shaping on the other side to match! The Manager offered the client a complimentary treatment, at the appropriate moment.

Making the offer of a complimentary treatment too soon, and the client would not have accepted it, too late and it would have been too late. This was not a situation where the Manager was able to replace the eyebrow! It was therefore one whereby the best had to be made out of a bad scenario.

Later, that therapist, who could so easily have lost her confidence in herself, her ability to wax, or perform any treatments, had her confidence restored by her caring Manager, who, by giving the therapist some time and practice showed her how to avoid making the same mistake again. The other valuable lesson learnt was how that Manager coped with the situation and although she could not bring the eyebrow back, thankfully defused the situation with the client before it had a chance to escalate and also managed to keep the client as a regular.

In today's world of beauty, some of the colleges do not offer or are unable to offer as much practical experience as the teachers would like and in this industry that is a disadvantage. It is the practical experiences that will help you gain confidence, smooth out areas that you are not strong on, help you learn some new methods, expand some of your college examples and build up speed.

You may decide that your plan is to work from home

For the mature student who is re-training in a new career, or perhaps beginning a new career now with the family grown up, the objective may be quite different to that of other students who just starting out on their first job.

If you are a student embarking on your career, you will have a different range of considerations to think about. Working for yourself is fine if you envisage that you will never want to work for someone in the future, and for the more mature student this could well be the case, but I would definitely not advise it if you are at the beginning of your working career and still around the age of 18, because you never know what life will throw at you and you may decide to, or you may have to, work for someone else at some stage.

Why does it matter? – because if you go straight from college to working for yourself at home, never having any salon experience, it will go against you if you apply for jobs in years to come, and you will be looked upon as possibly not being as "finished off". It may well be harder to find a job in a salon of your choice.

It is a concern of employers that if a person has never worked in a salon, they will not have the same understanding of salon problems, financial and practical, and they will also be concerned that you will be less likely to be happy to be guided in their preferred method of treatments.

I have known therapists that have worked for themselves all their lives and then needed to work for a salon because they have had divorce or some problem financially. It is often the case that they have no concept or understanding of how a salon works. Usually the difference is in the speed required to perform a treatment in a salon compared to a more relaxed approach in a home salon, or the costs involved for the owner to make the business work.

It is a contentious point but I can tell you that whatever you feel about this issue the fact is that I have had countless salons tell me that when looking for an experienced therapist they want salon experience and you will notice advertisements often state "salon experience" as one of their requirements.

Dealing with and understanding the business owner's perspective when going for your first or future jobs can help you progress in your career.

You can help yourself move forward by having some understanding of the trials and tribulations of the salon owner. By understanding a little about the business responsibility that the salon owner has you will appreciate some of the pressure they may be under. In turn, your employer will feel more supported by having someone working with them as opposed to against them and they will know that you understand the significance of the time and cost implications when they work out a future training programme or salary increase for you.

The average privately owned salon is quite cash poor despite outside appearances! The salons often offer a glamorous image and the clients may perceive many of the treatments as luxuries, although this thinking is changing in some areas.

The salon owner will need to cover the cost of your salary with the treatments that you are performing at least twice over. The more treatments you do and the more re-booking of clients you secure the more you are earning for the salon and the more you are likely to be able to negotiate better salaries, more training and commissions.

Many therapists say to me that the owner is charging large amounts for their treatments and that they, the therapists, are only getting a pittance. They feel they are being taken advantage of. (Obviously there are always exceptions to the rule, and not all of the salon owners are poor!)

You have to remember that the salon owner has built up the business and will have incurred marketing costs in getting the clients to the salon in the first place – they will have invested time and effort into building up that client base. They will have taken out loans and maybe mortgaged their houses to set up the business.

They will then have taken on new staff and in order to expand, they have to have new clients. Your coming into a salon and taking over existing clients is not growing the business, it is moving the business to you and so at that point you are an extra cost.

What the clients do not see, and the therapists are often unaware of, are the large overheads incurred in running a salon. At the time of writing this book – and this has not changed for the last 15 years at least – it is a very difficult market which to be a salon owner because, first of all the necessary perceived image for the clients is one of luxury.

The salons have to charge VAT to their clients on their treatments. This affects you indirectly and the salon owner directly.

1 The treatment price the salon charges the client includes VAT. This portion of the treatment price has to be paid to the VAT office. So the salon is not earning as much per treatment as you may think.

② Your commission is affected because the salon will need to deduct the VAT from the sale price of the treatments before calculating your percentage of commission.

The rent and rates in the high street are very high and many salons have to be in a high street location. The nature of the business means that salon owners have to open shift hours, evenings and weekends, in order to compete with other businesses and also to accommodate the busy lives of women who are predominantly still the main clients.

Maternity laws for the small salon owner are really hard, because they have to keep the job open while the therapist is having her baby and while she decides if she is coming back to work or not. Since the business is built on a personal service, the clients are not going to be happy to accept a 'Temp' very easily and therefore the salon owner is stuck. She cannot spread herself to cover the on-leave therapist's treatments and she cannot get in a temp for several months without upsetting the quality of her service.

In all of the treatment costs the salon owner has to take into account the running costs of the salon, staff and products used in the treatments.

By having a little bit of an understanding of the pressures of the salon owner you will find it easier to understand if you find yourself questioning how your commission is calculated or why you do not appear to have a reasonable hourly rate compared to the treatment cost.

9

Contracts and Job Offers

You have been offered a job, what next?

Congratulations, you have been offered a job. It is always a good idea to show appreciation for the offer but not actually accept until you have given it some thought overnight.

Sometimes it can be so exciting to be offered a job that you accept on the spot and then go home and realise there is something about the offer you are not keen on.

Or maybe when you are speaking to your parents or friends they ask you a question that you had not thought of.

If you are using an Agency, this is less of a problem because the Agency will have the experience and knowledge to make sure that you have thought through all possible concerns before they accept on your behalf.

The other advantage if using an Agency is that they can perhaps negotiate for you if you would like the job but would prefer different terms of agreement.

Of course you can always negotiate for yourself and this is fine. Just remember to negotiate without making it a war, so that you can keep the original job offer if you are not succeeding in improving it.

Once the offer has been made, the company will normally send you out an offer letter. Some companies will send this out first and others will send it out after making a verbal offer.

Offer Letters

This is a letter given to you confirming an offer of employment and will normally include the salary and the terms of commission the company is offering you, plus holiday entitlement, job title and the start date.

It is polite to write back with your acceptance and to telephone to acknowledge the letter and accept or decline the position. If you are going through an agency the agency will accept on your behalf and then arrange for you to ring the employer.

Keep a copy of this letter and put it in the file with your CV and training courses. You may need to refer to it one day if there is a discrepancy in your salary or even if you can't remember what your agreement is.

The offer letter may be sent by post or email.

Contracts of Employment

Contracts of Employment are issued to the employee by the employer. Some employers issue the contract immediately and others will wait until you have reached your probationary period, although the contract should be issued within two months of your start date and some probationary periods are up to three months.

The contract is to protect both parties and is a document to provide proof in the event of dispute that both parties understand and agree on the terms of employment.

It is a good idea to take the contract away and read it before signing it and returning it to the employer. You will normally be given two copies to sign, one for you to keep and one for the employer to keep.

The contract will normally include the salary details, and as these can change throughout your employment, there may be a clause allowing for salary reviews. Some salary details are often put in the offer letter only, for example commission rates. Contracts of employment do not always include details of the commission structure agreed with you at the "offer" stage. This is because the commission structures can change according to the incentives that are applicable to the company at any given time.

The contract may include things like disciplinary procedures, product training penalties, radius restrictions for new jobs, notice periods, staff conduct rules etc. It should confirm who your employer is and who you are and the date your employment commenced.

Often the Contract will include a clause that restricts where and when you can work in the event that you leave the salon's employment. For example your contract may say that you cannot work in another salon within a radius of 2 miles for a duration of 1 year after you leave the employment of the salon.

This clause should be considered because it must be reasonable in order to be enforced. It is to protect salons from people leaving and then enticing the salon's clients to a new business or competitor.

The distance restriction will be determined by the density of location with respect to business competition and the ability of the person to find work. This means that if you are in a rural area and there are miles between each village or business location, it is quite different to being in London where there are thousands of other salons you can work in.

Keep a copy of your Contract. People always forget to do this but it can be added to your file that you keep your CV in and is very useful for referring back to if there is a dispute and particularly when you want to hand in your notice. It will save asking embarrassing questions about notice periods etc.

What are Training Penalties?

This means that the company that employs you may offer to pay for you to go on training courses and in the event that you leave their employment before a designated time, then you will have to pay back all or a contribution towards the training costs.

This can often be a grey area because the cost of training is not always specified and so it is a good idea to find out how it is calculated before signing the contract.

When receiving training, make a note of the costs involved for each course you attend, so that you will always have the information to hand if a dispute arises or if you want to calculate at any time what the financial penalty will be if you decide to leave. There is a section at the back of this book for keeping that information to hand along with your course details.

Specifically, the costs to consider are: the actual cost of your training course; your salary while on that course; travel costs; accommodation costs if applicable.

The salon may have paid for the training itself or the training could be free. Is it just your salary that they are charging you for? They may have paid you a salary whilst you were on the course or they may not.

Your training penalty may include travel costs or accommodation.

Some salons will pay for the training but not the travel costs. Some will pay for everything.

Product houses vary in their charges to salons. Some do not charge their salons for training and some may allow for one or two people to train within the cost of their initial agreement with the salon, then charge for each employee after the initial two, for example.

Either way the salon will have paid for that training one way or another. Even if you perceive it to be free, you could be using their allowance up and so a cost is allocated to it.

Some salons will charge the full amount and some will make an allowance. Some salons do not impose a penalty or return of training costs at all.

Many salons will include the training penalty in the contract of employment but only use it at their discretion. If you have been an outstanding therapist and they want to show appreciation, they may decide not to exercise this right.

10

Aspirations, Career Directions

There are many different directions you can go into with your career; here are some ideas for career paths and jobs to aspire to.

Working on a Cruise Ship Spa. Beauty Therapist in Salon, Spa Therapist, Aesthetic Therapist in a Medical Clinic, Sales Consultant, Sales Executive or Account Manager on the Road, Marketing, Tele Sales, Trainer, Teacher Salon Management, Spa Management, Beauty Therapist working Abroad, Setting up your own Business, Front of House/Spa or Salon Reception.

Cruise Ships

This may change, but at the time of writing this book, you would need to be 21 years old and have a least one year's experience in a salon to work on a cruise ship.

The Cruise Ships are very good for your CV as future employers will know that you have worked in a sales-orientated atmosphere and will be quite used to selling products and not phased by commission structures. You will probably have gained a lot of confidence and experience during your time on board.

You will gain a vast amount of experience in a relatively short time and will probably learn to speak in public to large numbers. You will definitely learn to sell and you will gain a lot of confidence.

The Ships are not for everybody and many experienced therapists will tell you that they are glad they did it when they were younger because of the experience, and at 21 they didn't mind sharing with two or three others in a cabin, but wouldn't want to do this later in their careers.

One Therapist said that she loved it but couldn't get past the sea sickness!

Many say they have to stop because of bad backs from too much massage.

Another said it made her life, she loved every aspect of the travelling, the friendships she made, the training and she managed to save lots of money!

Spa Jobs

Many of the spas will have lots of positions for Newly Qualified Beauty Therapists, and this is a good way to get experience and training on products. Often there will be accommodation within the spa if you don't live near by.

Working in a spa is quite different from working in a high street salon and this should be taken into account when deciding on your long-term career plans. You may find that as a newly qualified you will be offered positions in spas catering for spa day visitors and your treatments may be pretty much mini versions of facials, manicure, pedicures and massage. From this starting point you can progress into the more exotic treatments, spas and locations.

In the spa world you are quite protected from the realities of working in a traditional beauty salon and you may find that there are some treatments or skills that you learnt at college that you are not practising. If it is your plan to one day work in a salon or even own your own salon then it is a good idea to make sure you have experience in a salon at some stage in your first few years after college.

Many salons will be nervous of taking on a Senior Therapist who has only ever worked in a spa because they will not have experienced the day-to-day issues that typical salons experience and they may not adjust to the smaller environment.

On the other hand, with the Spa type salons opening up in the high street, they may see a spa background as an advantage because they wish to create a spa experience for their clients while catering for everyday needs.

For someone who wishes to go right to the top of the tree in spa management, you have a perfect pedigree if you have only ever worked in spas and will probably be able to progress up the ladder with the spa that you join as a junior. There are different types of spas, some catering to the mainstream, novice spa-day visitors, to specialised spas catering to the spa sophisticates.

Many spas are in remote locations so you will need to take this into account. You may find that you will be happier in some of the locations if you can drive, because of greater choice of accommodation. A car will also mean that if you are living in the spa you will have flexibility to leave the grounds to go out during your days and evenings when you are not working.

Sales jobs

Sales in the beauty industry are divided up into Consultancy roles and Sales Executive roles, Telesales, Sales Management, Account Management.

Consultancy is generally selling in department stores, cosmetic counters in the airport, boutique cosmetic shops and specialised shops. In some spas and department stores sales is often combined with offering facials and limited treatments.

Sales executive roles generally involve working for product houses, selling to salons, spas, health clubs, hotels etc and will involve a lot of driving and travelling. You should expect to spend nights away from home and you will normally be required to run your own diary and often, home office. You will need to be self motivated, good at time management and have a clean driving licence. Progression to Management would be from Sales Executive to Area Management, Regional Management and then on to National Sales Management. Most sales companies will have stands at Beauty Shows and it will be part of your job to work at the shows on your company stand, nationwide and sometimes internationally.

Telesales. Until recently telesales in the Beauty Industry has been quite a gentle role, considered more of a support role to the direct sales force on the road and focussed on taking orders from account customers on the phone and solving order issues. We are now seeing the Beauty Industry Telesales roles becoming more in line with that of other industries and Direct Telesales are now expected in the new roles, giving you the opportunity to make the same commissions as traditionally sales people on the road would achieve. You would be expected to cold call and build up business contacts and achieve targets. The financial rewards can be as great, and you don't have to be on the road.

Training Jobs

Training roles can involve working for product houses, teaching salon staff how to use their products, or can perhaps involve going to colleges to train on products. Very often training positions are located within the companies' own training centres and so you will need to live within easy distance. Some companies have trainers that will visit their clients on site, to train on their product, in which case you would more than likely be based from home and be given an area to cover. Some companies will prefer you to have a training or teaching qualification and some will be happy to go on your work background.

Not all sales companies will want someone who has only ever been teaching in a school or college because they might consider that they do not have any commercial experience. You might like to consider taking a part-time "Training" qualification for example.

Teaching jobs

Teaching Beauty Therapy can be in Private or Technical Colleges, which can be large or small. Privately funded, publicly funded or a mixture of the two. Different colleges will specialise in different qualifications, for example, Cibtac, NVQ, ITEC to name a few, and when you embark on a Teacher Training course you might like to consider which qualification you would like to work towards teaching. Some colleges will train you to be a teacher while on the job working for them and others will require you to have the qualification beforehand. Some Colleges, when employing a teacher will look for someone with experience in the School Qualification that they offer, teaching is quite a flexible direction to work towards because you can go on to train to be an Assessor who marks the students for their final exams. Travelling to different colleges. You can work full time, part time and also as a "bank Teacher" on call. This gives you flexibility at times in your life where it might be useful to have flexible hours.

Medical Aesthetics

Working in Medical Aesthetics can be in Clinics, Medi Spas, Salons, Cosmetic Clinics. Treatments tend to be machine based such as IPL, Microdermabrasion, Laser Hair Removal or Medical Skin Peels.

There are salons that will offer these treatments alongside traditional beauty treatments and there are clinics that do not offer any beauty treatments. It is a good idea to consider this aspect because if you love your beauty treatments then you would miss them in a machine-based clinic.

You will no doubt be told by numerous people that you don't need electrolysis these days because of Laser Hair Removal. This is the case with some clinics and salons, but not always. It is an advantage to have both electrolysis and Laser. There are numerous examples of Therapists who have Electrolysis and Advanced Electrolysis being able to get even better salary packages and jobs because they can offer it all.

Temping

What is a Temp?

A "Temp" is a shortened version of the word "Temporary" and, as with other industries, the Beauty Industry often has a need for temporary therapists to work in salons to cover the periods when they are short of staff.

The Temp can be self-employed or can be on the payroll of an agency. Please see the section below for the different types of Temporary Agencies.

A "Temp" is possibly a better job for the experienced Therapist as the nature of the work means you often get thrown in at the deep end and the salon is hiring you because they need help and not to offer you support.

Once experienced, many Therapists choose to become "Temps" because they can control their own working hours and rates of pay if they work for themselves. Also, if they are in between jobs or don't want to commit to a permanent position for any reason then it is a very useful way to stay flexible while earning an income.

What is involved in becoming a Temp?

You will need to decide if you want to become a self-employed Temp, in which case you can find work from any of the agencies or by your own endeavours, or if you want to be a temp under the payroll of a dedicated temp agency so that that agency effectively becomes your employer.

If you go for the first option, you will need to phone up various agencies and put yourself on their books as available to work. They will need a CV which will include all the treatments and training that you have.

They will receive jobs from their clients who will ask them to match their requirements. For example, they may get a client asking for a Therapist who is trained on a particular product range and can work for two days for that week.

The agency will then ring you to see if you are available, agree a rate, and then book you in. You turn up at the client's for the allotted days.

Payment for Temping

If you are working for agencies on a self-employed basis, you would normally be paid directly by the client.

In the example of the job above it would be at the end of the two days' work. If your temp job with them was going to be for a more lengthy arrangement, for example several weeks, the payment day should be agreed in advance.

What Equipment will you need?

You will normally use the salon's equipment so it is unusual to have to buy your own. Very occasionally you may find that someone asks you to use your own manicure equipment, but this would definitely be the exception rather than the rule.

- ✪ You will need a couple of Uniforms if not more.
- ✪ A Mobile Telephone.
- ✪ A good map or A–Z
- ✪ If you travel by car – a Sat Nav will make life less stressful.

What Official Documents do you Need to be a Temp?

If you are working on a Self-Employed basis you will need a Registration Number from the Tax man to say you are officially Self-Employed.

You will also need to cover yourself with insurance. All salons should have insurance but you should have it as well if you are working for yourself.

Good places to get quotations for insurance for all Beauty Therapists (not just Temps) are:

BABTAC
www.babtac.com

The Federation of Holistic Therapists
www.fht.org. uk

Temps and Telephones

I would recommend you have a mobile dedicated to work only. This way when you answer it you know it is work related and you know that you need to be professional. You also know that if you are not in a position to speak freely and professionally then you should not answer it and pick up the message later, calling back when you are in the right place, mood, or situation. It means you can also put a message on it that is suitable to your work. I would look upon this as a business line that represents you. Think of yourself as a business.

The Cardinal Sin of Temps

Never have your mobile on while temping with salons. You are not being hired by them to spend their time on other people's business or your bookings. You should only check your messages and make calls in your own time and away from earshot of anyone else.

You may think that you have got away with it but the salon will be reporting back to the agency and neither the agency nor the salon will think you are professional if you commit this sin.

The Temporary Consultancy Agency options

There are two types of Temping Agency. The General Beauty Agency and the Dedicated Temp

Agency (see p. 130). The former work on permanent positions and will sometimes also offer temping jobs. These agencies are more likely to find you work on the basis that you work as a self-employed therapist on an hourly rate that you decide upon, in other words, you control what you hire yourself out for! This type of Agency will earn a fee for the days that you work and are paid by the salon, and the salon pays you your hourly rate directly. In the event that the salon you are temping in likes you a lot and asks you to become a full-time member of staff, they will have to pay this agency a finder's fee.

The second type of temping agency

These are the Dedicated Temping Agencies. You will effectively be working for that agency directly, except that you will only get paid when they find you temporary placements, so you are not on a regular income. These agencies will find you work in salons, department stores, events, rock concerts and shows. They will pay you wages for working for them. They agree rates with their clients which are in effect nothing to do with you. They have hired you to do a job, they pay you and they are your boss. You will be on their payroll and therefore you may not have to be registered as self-employed.

How does a Temp Agency earn it's money?

Both types of agency earn a commission for introducing you to the client. The first type of agency will probably charge the salon a daily/weekly rate which the salon will pay the agency directly and this is separate to your payment.

The second type of agency, that has you on the payroll, will receive a percentage of whatever rate or arrangement they have with the salon.

What makes a successful Temp?

The most successful temps – perhaps the ones that can demand the highest hourly rates – are never out of work and clients consistently ask the agencies for them. The Agency knows that they are excellent temps and so book them with their best clients. These temps are their first choice if there are several therapists available.

How do you make the most money as a temp?

- ✪ Consider yourself your own little business.
- ✪ Your presentation should be excellent.
- ✪ Maintain a high standard.
- ✪ Ensure you are always on time.
- ✪ Always turn up for the jobs.
- ✪ Never let the Agency down.
- ✪ Do not allow the salon to work a private deal against the Agency.
- ✪ Be prompt and efficient with your invoice.
- ✪ Keep your manner professional at all times.

✪ Be discreet, do not discuss other business in salons you temp in.

✪ Keep up-to-date with your accounts.

✪ Check out the journey and the hourly rate before agreeing to a temp job, it may not be practical or financially viable.

✪ Nurture your relationship with your agency.

If the agency knows you are consistently reliable, loyal and have respect for the salons, then they are going to look at you as their preferred therapist for booking, and they will have no hesitation in getting you the highest rate possible, turning down salons on your behalf that cannot pay the rate you want, safe in the knowledge that they will be able to find you temp work elsewhere because you are their star.

Whereas the temp that is always late, argumentative, gets lost on her way to the job, and looks scruffy will be the "last resort temp".

What is Self Employed?

Technically the term Self Employed means someone who works for themselves in various locations and is responsible for their own bookkeeping and accounts. They do not earn a salary as such from an employer, and are not actually employed by anyone. They would normally charge for the hours they work. When the Self-Employed Therapist is providing a service that they are being paid for it is normally by the hour or per contract and this person or company is technically her or his own client.

When you are working for someone on a self-employed basis they will want to know what your Self-Employed Registration Number is with the tax man. This means that the salon is protected because if they don't have it the tax man can come to them to claim tax for the period you were working for them.

What is an Invoice?

An invoice is simply a bill for your services. You would issue your bill to the salon so that they have a receipt and record of where the money they have paid you is allocated in their own Accounts.

You should have a copy of it for your own accounts.

You would show on your invoice the following information:
- ✪ Your Name and Address.
- ✪ Your Self-Employed Registration Number.
- ✪ The hours you have worked, if applicable.
- ✪ The dates you have worked.
- ✪ Your payment terms.

It may seem rather odd to you to put payment terms on your invoice because you are expecting to be paid on the day. However, there may be situations where you are paid at the end of the week, or where you are struggling to get your payment for one reason or another and therefore it is useful to have your terms on the invoice in case of dispute.

Don't be fearful about the paperwork. You do not have to have a complicated invoice, you could just have a duplicate note pad with you that you complete at the end of your temping day and that you issue to the client, keeping a copy for your accounts.

Keeping receipts

Keep all your receipts when Temping or working as a self-emplyed "mobile" therapist because you will be able to claim all sorts of things as expenses to reduce the tax you will have to pay. For example, your telephone that you use for business, your uniform, travel and all sorts of things that your accountant can advise you on.

Mobile Therapist

A mobile Therapist works for herself and will go to people's houses or companies to perform treatments. The mobile therapist will have her own equipment, price list and products and will be responsible for promoting herself.

The Fors and Againsts of being a Mobile Therapist

The pluses are that you are independent, you choose your own hours of work, you can earn more money per treatment than in a salon and you are your own boss.

For some Therapists the minuses are the irregular income, the cost and effort of travelling time and the fact that it can be harder to keep to the allotted time because of the nature of the personal service. Finally many Therapists find it a bit lonely and miss the team spirit in a salon.

Mobile Therapists and Hen Party/Event and Pamper Party Companies

There are various companies that promote Hen Parties and Pamper Parties and sometimes include services for Event companies. Some of these companies will also offer services to Businesses, such as massage to busy stressed executives at their place of work.

Most of these companies will use Mobile Therapists for the services they offer and pay the Therapist an hourly rate. There is the occasional one that will employ therapists itself and pay a salary but these are the exception rather than the rule.

Typically the Mobile Therapist will be registered with this services company and when the company has an event or party in their area the Mobile Therapist will be contacted to see if she is available and then booked in for that event.

The Mobile Therapist then arrives at the allocated event, normally with her own equipment, and performs the treatments.

Generally the Therapist is responsible for her own travel costs and arrangements and some companies will also expect the therapist to take her own towels, candles and products and portable couch.

The hourly rate is set by the services company and this will vary from company to company. The Therapist will be self employed with her own insurance.

Most of the treatments offered by these companies are massage and manicures but can sometimes include facials and others.

Of course you can also promote your own Pamper Parties and Hen Parties and not work for anyone.

11

Questions often asked by College Leavers and Students

Q What is a Trade Test?

As part of the interview, the salons will often ask you to perform some treatments.

This is so that the salon can assess how competent you are with your practical treatments and how you relate to the client.

Q All the adverts say they want experienced therapists, how do I get experience if they won't give me a chance?

This question is timeless, it is always a challenge for the students to find a job and for the question to be answered.

From every class of students leaving college there are always Therapists who find the roles. To meet your challenge, you have to decide to be one of those therapists.

As a Newly Qualified Therapist you may be feeling surprised by how difficult it is to get an interview, let alone your first job; maybe you feel disappointed or even angry. You thought the difficult part had just finished when you completed your college training and that you would just walk into a job.

In fact you now have the biggest challenge, you have to learn to promote yourself, become your own PR person. You are your own best advocate of yourself and you need to understand the game.

Ironically it is often harder for Newly Qualifieds when the economic market is tougher. One would have thought that it would be easier because of the lower salaries offered to Newly Qualifieds. But not so, it is often harder because the salons will be taking on staff because they need them and not because they are planning for the future. The salon will be wanting their new therapist to be able to offer treatments immediately. They may have been waiting to see if the market gets busy before they decide to take someone on and then there is an immediate urgency. Plus they may not be able to afford to take on anyone that is not covering their costs in the revenue they generate.

This means that Newly Qualifieds need to be pro-active, responsive and planned in their job search. Not only do you want to get a job but you want the right sort of job, with support and guidance. It would also be good to find a salon that is willing to commit to future training on new treatments and products. To achieve this you have to convince the salon that you are worth the investment. That you are genuine in your aspirations and you really want their job.

If you are not getting any interviews and job offers, you will need to make your own opportunities.

Have a look at your approach.

If necessary offer to work in local salons for a couple of days a week for nothing, it will be experience and you will be in the salon environment. It will give you the opportunity to prove to the salon owner that you are capable of doing the treatments. You can practice on the staff and you may learn some tips from the other therapists. If you make yourself useful you may find that if a vacancy becomes available they offer it to you.

Enrol onto courses to keep yourself motivated and in the loop, to meet other people and to add to your CV. Adding extra courses to your CV will show potential employers that you are enthusiastic and willing to help yourself. It will make you stand out from all the other Newly Qualified CVs that they get and it will be good for you to use your time effectively.

Get involved in voluntary work in hospitals, nursing homes, clubs, all the time meeting people and promoting yourself. So many Therapists are offered jobs because they have given a treatment to someone who has recommended them to someone else or who knows of a job going and recommends them.

Follow the guidelines in this book to fine-tune your presentation and submission on CVs and job approach.

When you do get an interview, make it count – give it 100% effort in your preparation.

Q I want to go on the ships and have to wait for one year before I am able to do that? Do I tell the salons I am approaching for interviews what my plans are? Am I being dishonest?

Unless the salon is looking for someone short term, you will be limiting your options in the number of salons that will be interested in you by mentioning that you will only stay with them for one year.

You will also be limiting yourself in your approach to the interview because you will not be approaching it with a long-term view and this may result in your not coming across with any conviction, and so you may not be offered the greatest package or training programme.

The answer is to keep an open mind because anything could happen in that year, you might change your mind on wanting to go away, you might be headhunted for some fabulous job you have not considered before, you might love the job you are in so much that you don't want to leave, you might get promoted to a Senior role and consider it better to stay. Or you might hate the job for reasons other than you can control and it would be a good time to go on the ships.

So the advice here is to keep your options open, approach your interview with 100% intention to give your all to the job. If in a year's time you want to go on the ships then you will consider it then. You have not lost anything because you have taken the opportunity of that job and it has had a year to convince you to stay. You have not been dishonest because you have always given the job 100% but for whatever reason you are now ready to make a move.

Or you could have the negative approach and go into a job thinking this will do for the meantime, not giving it anything and not getting anything back. Waste your year and then still decide at the end you don't want to go on the ships because you have just met your dream partner and then you have lost your first year.

So why not keep your options open and make every thing you do worthwhile? Don't limit yourself.

Q How long should I stay in my first job?

As long as possible is the simple answer, unless it is damaging your career or your health!

One Therapist worked for the same lady for 10 years. On the face of it, when she approached an Agency to move jobs, she looked like a dream candidate because she had stability and experience. On the other hand, she had had no formal training on anything new for 10 years and no variety and no experience in any other environment. Her salary was quite good and this gave her a problem because to move jobs she would have to take a drop in salary because of her lack of varied experience. To stay in the job meant she would not ever progress and she was unhappy. In this instance she would have been better off moving earlier in her career.

Q Do I admit I have a baby?

I have been asked this question many times by students who have been turned down for jobs and they are fearful that they are being rejected because they have a young child or baby. Some have actually been advised, wrongly I believe, not to tell the salon that they have a child.

I don't think it does make a difference that you have a child, I believe it is how you approach the interview that makes the difference.

If your approach to the interview is giving the impression that your having a baby is a hindrance, or a problem, then that is what will come across in the interview. It is better not to make an issue of it, be proud that you have a baby and explain that you have child cover arranged and all is under control.

If the salon owner can see that you are organised and calm about it then they will not see it as an issue to be concerned about.

Q What is Commission?

Commission is paid by salons, normally over and above your basic salary. There are many different types of commission packages.

Commission can be paid out on product sales, or on the amount of treatments that you do, or on both products and treatments. Commission is a percentage of the price of your treatment or product sales that you earn over and above your normal salary.

For example, you might be offered your basic salary of say £6.50 per hour plus 10% on treatments and 5% on products sales.

Some salons will put a proviso in that you have to earn twice the equivalent of your salary before you go onto commission. Some will give you a turnover figure that you have to achieve before you go onto commission, for example: Once you have achieved £500 worth of treatments in a week you are eligible for commission of 10% on any treatments thereafter.

Most salons will calculate your commission by calculating your turnover on treatments, deducting the VAT, and calculating your commission percentage from the figure left. So for this example your new employer has offered you a job with a basic salary plus 10% commission on all treatments, to be calculated and paid out on a weekly basis.

For this example I have used 17.5% as the VAT figure but you should check this when the time comes for you to calculate as this figure can change.

Some salons do not offer any commission at all, particularly spas.

Commission can make quite a difference to your income and so it is worth understanding it and making it work for you.

Q What has VAT to do with Commission?

The VAT that I referred to in the previous paragraph stands for Value Added Tax. All businesses that have an income level over a certain amount have to charge their clients VAT and they have to pay that VAT to the tax man. Therefore they have to take it off your commission figure because it is a tax that has been added on to the treatment costs in effect by the tax man, who uses the salon owner as a vehicle for getting some money. Therefore the salon owner cannot give you commission on that part of the treatment cost because it is not theirs to give.

Q Will the salon give me a uniform?

Uniforms are sometimes provided by the salon and sometimes not.

If the salon supplies your uniform, when you leave you must return it to them.

Even if you provide your own uniform it is still reasonable for the salon owner to expect you to look smart and clean and to adhere to the colours that they request and the colour of shoes that they prefer you to wear.

Q **What has it got to do with a salon if I smoke?**
Do they have the right to ask me?

It just doesn't work in this industry.

Your judgement and dedication to the industry will
be in question before you even open your mouth so
you will have to work harder to overcome that
negative. You will smell of it.

I have had therapists turned down for jobs because
the salon owners can smell smoke on them at
interview, even though they have told me they
don't smoke.

I could go on and on about how the smell of smoke
affects clients when giving a treatment, but that's
not what this book is about. It is your guide to
getting a job and getting the best career in your
industry.

I can only give you the facts and then it's your
choice.

Whether it is right or wrong to ask, the fact is you
will dramatically reduce your chances of a good
job if you smoke.

12

Extract from my next book to be published

"Getting a Job in the Beauty Industry Advanced Considerations: Recruitment Secrets for Advanced Beauty Therapists"

Many years ago a candidate that a colleague of mine was working with came on the books of the beauty agency and wanted to work in Sales in some capacity. A position came up with a product house for a counter sales person in a department store. It was a nice company and a job with good prospects and my colleague thought it would be an ideal opportunity for this candidate, who was moving to the area. My colleague, who will remain anonymous, will forgive me for saying that she was a very pedantic person and very thorough. She was pleased with herself for finding this particular match and went to great pains to ensure that the candidate discussed any concerns that she had before the interview and even gloated to me how perfect the match was the week before the interview! We had worked with the client before and were comfortable that we knew everything we needed to know about the job, the candidate was very happy and my colleague was smugly confident that this was "in the bag"!

The day before the interview the candidate phoned my colleague and without preamble went straight into a challenge, followed by a threat. She said in a very accusatory voice, "I want to know if these people are interviewing me because they feel sorry for me and if they are wasting my time I will sue."

My colleague was bemused to say the least, and asked why anyone would feel sorry for her. The reply came back that it was because she was only four feet tall. My colleague reassured her this would not be the case and put the phone down.

Immediately she picked it up again and phoned me in a high-pitched rather hysterical panic. Should she phone the product house and discuss it? Would it be a problem? Does this person have a personality disorder to suddenly come out with it now and, worst of all, it slowly dawned on her, were the counters in department stores not about 4 foot tall !! ???

An agency has to look at it from both the clients' and the candidates' perspectives. Whichever way we looked at this, the situation looked bleak. We had to decide whether it was ethical to phone the company and ask them exactly how tall their counters were and did they have any height issues? And risk them saying four foot and then having to phone the candidate back, knowing that she would probably find a reason to sue for that. If they did not have any issues then we did not want to lose her the opportunity for the interview by frightening them off, because we clearly had an "I know my rights person on our hands".

We took the cowardly approach and did nothing, on the basis that if she was too short to see over the counter and if it was an issue, then they could make the decision. We crossed our fingers and hoped that she would have forgotten her vitriolic mood. If she did not get the job, we reassured ourselves, would be for reasons other than her height.

This is where fate stepped in! She went for her interview, unfortunately the person who was to interview her was called away just before she arrived as one of their parents had died unexpectedly.

Another person stepped in valiantly to do the interview and apologised for the absence of their colleague.

My colleague received a wild and furious phone call from the candidate accusing, threatening and confirming that she was right, they had clearly not wanted to interview her, the person who she was meant to see could not even be bothered to show up for the interview, and the person she did see clearly had no information about the job to discuss. She ranted and raved and said that she was going to sue and she would never work for such a company that was so anti-disabled, did not want to go for any further interviews, and would not take the job if they offered it, then slammed the phone down.

Totally floored at this stage and having not yet spoken to the company involved, my colleague phoned to find out how they felt the interview went and found out that sadly the boss had been called away, but his second in command had been available to interview and they felt it went very well.

Two days later my colleague received a phone call from the company saying they really liked this candidate and would like to offer her the job!

Book Two also goes into more depth about the issues you may come across when job searching, and the problems you may encounter when you have been in the industry for a little while. It will include ways to overcome obstacles and to consider how changes in your personal life may make it necessary to rethink your career. With more real-life experiences and packed full of tips and support.

13

Your Record of Training Courses

Course Name: ....

Dates To–From/Duration: ....

Location: ....

Course Cost: ....

Travel Costs: ....

Expenses: ....

Salary Paid: ....

Accommodation Costs: ....

Total Costs: ....

* * *

Course Name: ....

Dates To–From/Duration: ....

Location: ....

Course Cost: ....

Travel Costs: ....

Expenses: ....

Salary Paid: ....

Accommodation Costs: ....

Total Costs: ....

Course Name: ....
Dates To–From/Duration: ....
Location: ....
Course Cost: ....
Travel Costs: ....
Expenses: ....
Salary Paid: ....
Accommodation Costs: ....
Total Costs: ....

* * *

Course Name: ....
Dates To–From/Duration: ....
Location: ....
Course Cost: ....
Travel Costs: ....
Expenses: ....
Salary Paid: ....
Accommodation Costs: ....
Total Costs: ....

Course Name: ....

Dates To–From/Duration: ....

Location: ....

Course Cost: ....

Travel Costs: ....

Expenses: ....

Salary Paid: ....

Accommodation Costs: ....

Total Costs: ....

* * *

Course Name: ....

Dates To–From/Duration: ....

Location: ....

Course Cost: ....

Travel Costs: ....

Expenses: ....

Salary Paid: ....

Accommodation Costs: ....

Total Costs: ....

Course Name: ....

Dates To–From/Duration: ....

Location: ....

Course Cost: ....

Travel Costs: ....

Expenses: ....

Salary Paid: ....

Accommodation Costs: ....

Total Costs: ....

* * *

Course Name: ....

Dates To–From/Duration: ....

Location: ....

Course Cost: ....

Travel Costs: ....

Expenses: ....

Salary Paid: ....

Accommodation Costs: ....

Total Costs: ....

Course Name: ....

Dates To–From/Duration: ....

Location: ....

Course Cost: ....

Travel Costs: ....

Expenses: ....

Salary Paid: ....

Accommodation Costs: ....

Total Costs: ....

* * *

Course Name: ....

Dates To–From/Duration: ....

Location: ....

Course Cost: ....

Travel Costs: ....

Expenses: ....

Salary Paid: ....

Accommodation Costs: ....

Total Costs: ....

Lightning Source UK Ltd.
Milton Keynes UK
06 May 2010

153845UK00001B/6/P